BrightRED Revision

Higher COMPUTING

Alan Williams

First published in 2008 by:

Bright Red Publishing Ltd
6 Stafford Street
Edinburgh
EH3 7AU

Reprinted in 2012

A CIP record for this book is available from the British Library

ISBN 978-1-906736-01-9

With thanks to Ken Vail Graphic Design, Cambridge (layout) and Ivor Narmand (copy-edit)

Cover design by Caleb Rutherford – eidetic

Illustrations by Beehive Illustration (Martin Sanders), Phillip Burrows and Sylvie Poggio Artists Agency (Laura Martinez).

Acknowledgements

Every effort has been made to seek all copyright holders. If any have been overlooked then Bright Red Publishing will be delighted to make the necessary arrangements.

Bright Red Publishing would like to thank Simon Belcher/Alamy for permission to reproduce the photograph on page 9 and Emily Hooton for permission to reproduce the photographs on pages 107 and 116.

Printed and bound in the UK by W & G Baird Ltd.

CONTENTS

Look at all other Topics tomorrow (Mon 4th)

1 Higher Course
Syllabus and Assessment   4

2 Computer Systems
Data Representation 1   6
Data Representation 2   8
Computer Structure 1   10
Computer Structure 2   12
System Performance   14
Networking 1   16
Networking 2   18
Computer Software 1   20
Computer Software 2   22
Hardware – Input Devices   24
Hardware – Output Devices   26
Hardware – Storage Devices   28
Typical Tasks   30
Exam-Style Questions   32
Answers   34

3 Software Development
Software Development Process – Introduction and Personnel   36
Software Development Process – Analysis   38
Software Development Process – Design   40
Software Development Process – Implementation   42
Software Development Process – Testing   44
Software Development Process – Documentation and Evaluation   46
Software Development Process – Maintenance   48
Languages and Environments 1   50
Languages and Environments 2   52
High-Level Programming Language Constructs 1   54
High-Level Programming Language Constructs 2   56
Standard Algorithms   58
Exam-Style Questions   60
Answers   62

4 Artificial Intelligence
The Development of Artificial Intelligence 1   64
The Development of Artificial Intelligence 2   66
Applications of Artificial Intelligence 1   68
Applications of Artificial Intelligence 2   70
Search Techniques   72
Knowledge Representation   74
Exam-Style Questions   76
Answers   78

5 Computer Networking
Network Protocols 1   80
Network Protocols 2   82
Network Applications   84
Networks – Social and Ethical Issues   86
Networks – Security and Threats   88
Network Protection   90
Data Transmission and Network Switching 1   92
Data Transmission and Network Switching 2   94
Wireless Networking   96
Internet Connections   98
Exam-Style Questions   100
Answers   102

6 Multimedia Technology
The Development Process   104
Bit-mapped Graphics Data   106
Digitised Sound Data   108
Vector Graphics Data and Synthesised Sound Data   110
Video Data   112
Developments in Technology   114
Exam-Style Questions   116
Answers   118

7 Coursework Task
Outline and Guidance   120

Index   122

3

SYLLABUS AND ASSESSMENT

INTRODUCTION

This book is intended to present the content for the Higher Computing course in a concise and digestible format. It does not attempt to go into the detail that would be found in a full-blown textbook. However, it does cover the important examinable concepts, and it addresses frequently asked questions in a way that is more manageable for the student. If you can learn all the information in this book, then you will be well placed to tackle Higher Computing.

Important words and phrases are highlighted in the text to stress terms that are frequently asked to be explained in the exam or are often explained badly by students.

SYLLABUS

The Higher course consists of three units. Unit 1 and Unit 2 are mandatory, and Unit 3 is chosen from three optional units.

Compulsory Units	Optional Units (one from these three)
Computer Systems	Artificial Intelligence
Software Development	Computer Networking
	Multimedia Technology

Given below is an outline of the content of the Higher Computing units. This is merely an outline to give you an idea of what to expect, and not a detailed syllabus.

Computer Systems

The representation of data (numbers, text and graphics) in a computer system.
The structure and functions of a computer system and the factors that affect performance.
A description of networks, including LANs, WANs, topologies, client/server, peer to peer, network hardware and legal acts.
Computer software, including operating-system functions, utility programs and viruses.
Characteristics of computer hardware, including accuracy, capacity, speed and cost and the selection of suitable hardware to support typical tasks.

Software Development

The software development process through the stages of analysis, design, implementation, testing, documentation, evaluation and maintenance.
Description of high-level languages (variables, control constructs, procedures and functions).
Languages and environments (procedural, declarative, event-driven, scripting).
Standard algorithms (finding maximum and minimum, linear search, counting occurrences).

Artificial Intelligence

The development of artificial intelligence.
Applications and uses of artificial intelligence.
Search techniques.
Knowledge representation.

Computer Networking

Network protocols (Telnet, HTTP, FTP, SMTP, TCP/IP).
Description of web pages using HTML and WML.
Social, ethical, commercial and legal implications of networks.
Threats to network security and protection methods.
Methods of data transmission.

contd

SYLLABUS contd

Multimedia Technology

The development process for multimedia applications.

Bit-mapped graphics data.

Digitised sound data.

Video data.

Vector graphics data and synthesised sound data.

Multimedia data-compression techniques.

Implications of the use of multimedia technology.

ASSESSMENT

Your overall grade in Higher Computing is determined from your performance in the exam and the coursework task. The exam is allocated 140 marks, and the coursework task is allocated 60 marks. Clearly, the exam contributes a 70% majority of the total marks – but do not take the coursework task lightly, as your performance in 30% of the assessment can make a significant difference to your overall grade. The coursework task will be dealt with in some detail at the end of this book.

Unit Assessment

Each unit has a theory assessment and a practical checklist of skills that you have to demonstrate. Each theory assessment is a 45-minute multiple-choice test in which the pass mark is 12 out of 20. You will be given fairly short tasks developed in your own school to demonstrate the practical skills. If you fail an assessment, then you have a second chance in a re-test.

> **DON'T FORGET**
>
> You have to pass the unit assessments to complete the course, but they do not count towards your overall marks.

THE EXAM

Time and structure

The exam lasts 2 hours 30 minutes and is structured into three sections.

Section	Units Examined	Marks	Ratio of KU:PS
Section 1	Computer Systems and Software Development	30	2:1
Section 2	Computer Systems and Software Development	60	1:2
Section 3	Optional Unit	50	1:2

Section 1

Short-response questions on Computer Systems and Software Development. The ratio of Knowledge and Understanding questions to Problem-Solving questions is roughly 2:1.

Section 2

Extended-response questions on Computer Systems and Software Development. The ratio of Knowledge and Understanding questions to Problem-Solving questions is roughly 1:2.

Section 3

Extended-response questions on the Optional Unit. The ratio of Knowledge and Understanding questions to Problem-Solving questions is roughly 1:2.

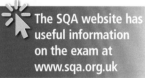

> The SQA website has useful information on the exam at www.sqa.org.uk

LET'S THINK ABOUT THIS

The overall grade is made up of an exam (70%) and a coursework task (30%). Past-paper exam questions will give you a feel for the style of questions and the content you can expect in your exam.

> **DON'T FORGET**
>
> Every year, dozens of students mistakenly attempt to answer **all** three options in Section 3 in the exam. Remember, you only answer one option in Section 3 – Artificial Intelligence **or** Computer Networking **or** Multimedia Technology.

DATA REPRESENTATION 1

UNITS

> Look up other units that are used in computing by entering the keywords 'Petabyte' and 'Exabyte' into a search engine.

Term		
Bit	A binary digit	1 or 0
Byte	A group of 8 bits	e.g. 10011101
Kilobyte (Kb)	2^{10} bytes	1024 bytes
Megabyte (Mb)	2^{20} bytes	1 048 576 bytes
Gigabyte (Gb)	2^{30} bytes	1 073 741 824 bytes
Terabyte (Tb)	2^{40} bytes	1 099 511 627 776 bytes

WHOLE NUMBERS

Whole numbers are the set of numbers 0, 1, 2, 3 …

These numbers are stored in a computer in binary, which is a number system based on powers of 2. The example below shows how the number 35 491 is stored in 16-bit binary.

32 768	16 384	8192	4096	2048	1024	512	256	128	64	32	16	8	4	2	1
1	0	0	0	1	0	1	0	1	0	1	0	0	0	1	1

32 768 + 2048 + 512 + 128 + 32 + 2 + 1 = **35 491**

Conversion of Whole Numbers to Binary

2	41 800	
2	20 900	R 0
2	10 450	R 0
2	5225	R 0
2	2612	R 1
2	1306	R 0
2	653	R 0
2	326	R 1
2	163	R 0
2	81	R 1
2	40	R 1
2	20	R 0
2	10	R 0
2	5	R 0
2	2	R 1
2	1	R 0
2	0	R 1

Answer 1010001101001000

To convert a whole number to binary, the number is repeatedly divided by **two** until **zero** is reached. The binary number is then obtained from the remainders (read from bottom to top).

The example alongside shows how to convert the number 41 800 into 16-bit binary.

Range of Numbers

The formula 2^N represents the number of different binary numbers that can be represented in N bits.

The range of whole numbers that can be represented in N bits is therefore $0\ldots2^N - 1$, since the smallest value is 0.

For example, 16 bits can store 2^{16} numbers. This gives a range of numbers from 0 to $2^{16} - 1$ $(0\ldots65\ 535)$.

> **DON'T FORGET**
>
> It is a common mistake to think that 2^N is the largest whole number in N bits. The largest whole number in N bits is $2^N - 1$ because there are 2^N numbers, starting with zero.

INTEGERS

Integers are the numbers $\ldots-3, -2, -1, 0, 1, 2, 3\ldots$

Two's complement is used to store integers in a computer system. This course is concerned only with 8-bit two's complement, in which the most significant bit represents -128 and the remaining bits are the same as for whole numbers.

The example below shows how the number -73 is stored in 8-bit two's complement.

−128	64	32	16	8	4	2	1
1	0	1	1	0	1	1	1

$-128 + 32 + 16 + 4 + 2 + 1 = -73$

contd

INTEGERS contd

The table below shows how to find the two's complement for −73 from the two's complement of 73.

−128	64	32	16	8	4	2	1	
0	1	0	0	1	0	0	1	73
1	0	1	1	0	1	1	0	Flip 1s and 0s
						+	1	Add 1
1	0	1	1	0	1	1	1	−73

> **DON'T FORGET**
>
> Remember to add the 1 after flipping the 1s and 0s when converting a positive two's complement number to a negative.

The table below shows the range of numbers in 8-bit two's complement.

	−128	64	32	16	8	4	2	1	
Largest	0	1	1	1	1	1	1	1	127
Smallest	1	0	0	0	0	0	0	0	−128

REAL NUMBERS

Real numbers include decimal fractions as well as integers.
Examples of real numbers are 7, −2, 518.2, −8.127, 5, 823, 0.0475.

Floating-point representation is used to store real numbers in a computer system in a manner similar to standard-form notation. The floating-point number is made up of a mantissa and an exponent. The mantissa holds the significant figures of the number, and the exponent holds the power.

For example: Mantissa $\rightarrow 0.11011 \times 2^{011} \leftarrow$ Exponent

Advantage

Floating-point notation allows very large and very small numbers to be stored in a small number of bits.

Disadvantage

Accuracy is lost, since the mantissa only gives the number to a certain amount of significant figures.

The example on the right illustrates a floating-point number with a 5-bit mantissa and 3-bit exponent.

Mantissa						Exponent		
$\frac{1}{2}$	$\frac{1}{4}$	$\frac{1}{8}$	$\frac{1}{16}$	$\frac{1}{32}$		4	2	1
1	1	0	1	1		0	1	1

$$= \frac{1}{2} + \frac{1}{4} + \frac{1}{16} + \frac{1}{32} \qquad = 2 + 1$$
$$= \frac{27}{32} \qquad\qquad = 3$$
$$= 0.84375$$

$$= 0.84375 \times 2^3$$
$$= 6.75$$

Range and Accuracy of Floating-Point Numbers

Increasing the number of bits assigned to the mantissa increases the accuracy of the numbers represented.

Increasing the number of bits assigned to the exponent increases the range of numbers that can represented.

LET'S THINK ABOUT THIS

The following units are used widely in the Higher course, and it is essential to know their exact definition: Kb, Mb, Gb.

The scope of this course covers conversion of whole numbers to binary and vice versa up to 32-bit numbers.

Two's complement is used to store integers, and floating-point representation is used to store real numbers.

DATA REPRESENTATION 2

TEXT

Text in a computer system is represented by using a binary code for each character.

ASCII and Unicode are two standards that have been developed for text representation to allow textual data to be transferred between different computer programs.

Parity bit | 7-bit code

11000001

Parity bit set to 1 to give odd parity, i.e. three 1s.

11000001

Parity bit set to 0 to give odd parity, i.e. five 1s.

01010111

ASCII (American Standard Code for Information Interchange)

The ASCII system represents each character in 8 bits. The most significant bit is called a parity bit and is used for error-checking, and the remaining 7 bits are used to encode the character.

The example shows how the character 'A' is represented in ASCII.

This allows for $2^7 = 128$ different codes. This is sufficient to represent 26 upper-case and 26 lower-case letters, a few dozen punctuation characters, the symbols for the digits 0, 1, 2, 3...9 and control characters. (Control characters are special non-printing characters used for purposes such as Return, Tab and End of file.)

Parity Bit

The first bit of a byte is used as a parity bit, which is used to detect errors in the transmission of single characters. If odd parity is used, then the parity bit is set to 1 or 0 so that the total number of 1s in the byte is an odd number.

The receiver checks the parity of the byte. If it is not odd, then the receiver requests that the data be retransmitted.

Unicode

The Unicode system uses 16 bits to encode each character, which allows for $2^{16} = 65\ 536$ codes. This large number of codes allows the Unicode system to represent characters in foreign languages throughout the world, such as Japanese or Arabic.

Comparison of ASCII and Unicode

- ASCII requires less storage than Unicode, since ASCII uses 1 byte to store each character whereas Unicode uses 2 bytes.

- Unicode can store $2^{16} = 65\ 536$ characters whereas ASCII can only store $2^7 = 128$ characters.

DON'T FORGET

The ASCII system represents 128 characters and **not** 256 characters, since 1 bit is used for a parity check so that only 7 bits of the byte are used for the character code.

GRAPHICS

Bit-Mapped Graphics

This type of graphics stores the image as colour codes for a two-dimensional grid of pixels. The term pixel comes from *pictures element* and is the dots that make up the graphic.

Bit Depth

The number of bits that are used to code the colour of each pixel is called the bit depth.

An image using 1-bit depth will only be able to represent two colours – usually black and white.

An image using 24-bit depth (true colour) will be able to represent $2^{24} = 16\ 777\ 216$ colours.

(True colour represents the limit to the number of colours that the human eye can recognise.)

Resolution

The resolution is the size of the pixels and is usually measured in dots per inch (dpi).

High-resolution graphics has a large number of small pixels.

Low-resolution graphics has a small number of large pixels.

DON'T FORGET

The number of colours that can be represented in a bit depth of N bits is derived from the formula 2^N. This notion of N bits giving rise to 2^N codes will appear repeatedly in this course.

contd

GRAPHICS contd

300 dpi, 256 colours

5 inches

4 inches

Calculation of Storage Requirements of Bit-Mapped Graphics

The example alongside shows the calculation for the storage requirements of a bit-mapped graphic in megabytes.

Storage requirements
$$= 5 \times 4 \times 300 \times 300 \times 8 \text{ bits } (2^8 = 256)$$
$$= 14\ 400\ 000 \text{ bits}$$
$$= 1\ 800\ 000 \text{ bytes}$$
$$= 1.72 \text{ Mb}$$

Vector Graphics

This type of graphic stores the image as a list of objects, each object being described by its attributes.

For example, the image shown below consists of Rectangle, Circle and Line objects.

Each object is stored by its attributes:

e.g. Line: start x, start y, end x, end y, line colour, line thickness and so on.
Circle: centre x, centre y, radius, fill colour, line colour and so on.
Rectangle: start x, start y, length, breadth, fill colour, line colour and so on

Comparison of Bit-Mapped Graphics and Vector Graphics

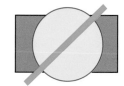

- Bit-mapped graphics can be edited in fine detail at the pixel level, but vector graphics are edited by changing the attributes of objects.

- Bit-mapped graphics have large storage requirements to store all the pixels, but it requires much less storage for vector graphics to store codes for objects and their attributes.

- Bit-mapped graphics are stored at a fixed resolution, but vector graphics are resolution-independent. Therefore vector graphics can take advantage of a high-resolution output device such as a printer, but bit-mapped graphics cannot.

- Bit-mapped graphics become jagged when enlarged, but vector graphics do not since the resolution is not fixed.

- Parts of a bit-mapped graphic cannot be separated without leaving blank areas of pixels, but in vector graphics overlapping objects can be separated.

FILE COMPRESSION

File compression is used to reduce the size of a file. The amount of compression will depend upon the type of file, but the compressed file can be several times less than the original file. The compressed file must be decompressed to the original file before it can be used.

There are two main advantages of compressing a file:

1 Less storage space is required for the compressed file.

2 The compressed file can be transmitted more quickly over a network.

 Look at the website www.winzip.com to find out more about file compression.

LET'S THINK ABOUT THIS

ASCII and Unicode are two standards for representing text in a computer system.

ASCII stores each character in 8 bits, and Unicode stores each character in 16 bits.

LEARN the calculation for the storage requirements of bit-mapped graphics, as it is always asked somewhere in the exam.

COMPUTER STRUCTURE 1

WHY BINARY?

A computer is described as a **two-state** device because data is represented by on or off (1 or 0).

There are several advantages of a computer representing data in 1s and 0s.

- Simpler circuitry since only two voltage levels are required to represent 1 and 0.

- Calculations are simpler since there are only rules for performing addition with combinations of 1s and 0s (0+0, 1+0, 0+1, 1+1).

- The system is more tolerant to fluctuations in voltage since a degraded 1 is still a voltage and recognised as a 1 and not a 0. If 10 voltage levels were used, then this would be more of a problem.

- Storing data on backing store devices is relatively simple since there are two states to be represented – for example, two states of magnetisation on a magnetic disc.

COMPUTER ORGANISATION

Stored Program Concept

A computer solves a problem by storing a set of instructions (a program) in memory that are then fetched and executed one at a time to solve a problem. This is called the Stored Program Concept.

Modern computers operate using a stored program concept.

Simple Structure of a Computer

The diagram below shows the basic components of a computer system.

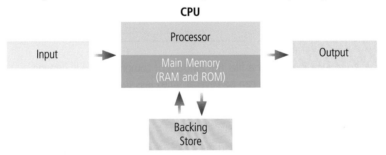

DON'T FORGET

The simple structure of a computer system and the function of its basic components are fundamental to the more detailed analysis that follows later in this course. Therefore it is essential to make sure that they are studied fully at this stage.

The CPU (Central Processing Unit)

The CPU is made up of a processor microchip and main memory chips.

Processor

The processor is responsible for fetching instructions held in main memory and executing them one at a time.

Main Memory

Main memory stores the programs and data that are currently being executed. It consists of RAM and ROM.

RAM (Random-Access Memory)

RAM is volatile (loses its contents when the power is switched off).

RAM can be read from and written to. When a program is loaded from the hard disc to be run, the program instructions are written into RAM.

contd

COMPUTER ORGANISATION contd

There are two types of RAM: **static** RAM and **dynamic** RAM.

Static RAM keeps its contents so long as power is maintained to the chip, but dynamic RAM requires to be refreshed every few milliseconds by rewriting its contents as well as power being supplied. Dynamic RAM has simpler circuitry than static RAM and needs less power. Consequently, dynamic RAM is cheaper than static RAM. The main advantage of static RAM over dynamic RAM is that it has faster access.

ROM (Read-Only Memory)

ROM is non-volatile (keeps its contents when the power is switched off).

The programs in ROM are put into the chip when it is manufactured and are permanent. The instructions in ROM can be read by the processor, but they are never written to.

A small part of the operating system which is executed at start-up, called the BIOS (Basic Input/Output System), is stored in ROM.

PROM (Programmable Read-Only Memory)

This is a type of ROM chip that is manufactured with empty storage locations that can then be permanently programmed by the user.

EPROM (Erasable Programmable Read-Only Memory)

This is a type of ROM chip whose contents can be erased by a process involving ultra-violet light. This is useful in the development of ROM chips.

DON'T FORGET

There are a lot of acronyms used in this course. Make sure that you know them **all**, but also remember that expanding an acronym is not sufficient to answer a question such as: 'What is the function of RAM?'

PERIPHERAL DEVICES

Input Devices

These are devices used to enter data into the CPU.

Examples of input devices are: keyboard, mouse, digital camera, scanner.

Output Devices

These are devices used to output data from the CPU.

Examples of output devices are: monitor, printer, plotter.

Backing Store Devices

These are devices used to store program and data files permanently. Since RAM is volatile, data files need to be saved to a backing store device before power is switched off, or else the data is lost.

Examples of backing store devices are: hard disc drive, magnetic disc drive, DVD drive, USB stick, floppy disc.

Look at the website www.pcworld.co.uk to research the variety of input, output and backing store devices that are available.

 LET'S THINK ABOUT THIS

When answering a question, make sure that you use any technical terms that are appropriate. For example, when describing vector graphics, it is better to talk about objects and their attributes and not shapes and their features.

The coursework task in Higher Computing requires knowledge of input, output and backing store devices. You will need to research actual devices in terms of characteristics such as speed, capacity, cost and accuracy (see under 'Hardware' later in this section).

COMPUTER STRUCTURE 2

DETAILED STRUCTURE

The processor consists of a Control Unit, Arithmetic Logic Unit (ALU), and Registers.

Control Unit

The control unit is responsible for initiating the fetching, decoding and execution of instructions by sending out signals to other parts of the computer system.

ALU (Arithmetic and Logic Unit)

The ALU carries out arithmetic operations (+, −, *, /) and logical operations such as AND, OR, NOT and so on.

Processor Registers

Registers are individual storage locations on the processor which hold an instruction, data or the address of a memory location.

The Instruction Register (IR) holds the instruction that is currently being executed by the processor.

The Accumulator (A) is a data register which holds the accumulated results of calculations performed in the ALU.

The Program Counter (PC) is a register which holds the address of the main memory location storing the next instruction to be executed by the program.

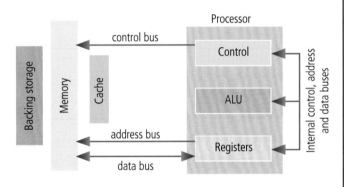

> **DON'T FORGET**
>
> A processor register holds only a single item of data. Do not confuse this with main memory, which holds data items in millions of memory locations.

PROCESSOR BUSES

The CPU has buses, which are multiple lines that connect the processor and main memory and are used to transfer data and send signals between them.

Data Bus

This bus is used to transfer data between main memory and the processor. It is a two-way bus, since data can be transferred from a memory location to the processor and vice versa. Early computers had a data bus that was eight lines wide and transferred eight bits in a single operation. Modern desktop computers will typically have a 32-bit data bus. The number of bits that the processor transfers in one operation is called the **wordsize**.

Address Bus

This bus is used to specify the address of the memory location that is to be read from or written to. This bus is a one-way bus, since the processor will use it to specify which memory location it is going to use but the reverse does not apply. Early computers had an address bus that was 16 lines wide. Modern desktop computers will typically have a 32-bit address bus.

Control Bus

Each of the control bus lines has a specific function. Some control bus lines are described below:

Read: a signal down this line is used to initiate a memory read operation which reads the contents of a memory location into the processor.

contd

PROCESSOR BUSES contd

Write: a signal down this line is used to initiate a memory write operation which writes an item of data from the processor into a memory location.

Clock: the clock line sends a regular series of pulses into the processor to synchronise events. The time interval between pulses is called a clock cycle. For example, a memory read or a memory write takes place in one clock cycle.

Reset: a signal down this line causes the computer to stop execution of the current program and then reboot.

Interrupt: peripheral devices such as printers can send a signal on the interrupt line into the processor when they require attention. This causes the processor to save the state of the processor registers so that it can return to where it was after dealing with the interrupting device.

NMI (Non-Maskable Interrupt): this is an interrupt that requires serious attention, such as power failure, and cannot be ignored.

DON'T FORGET

The control bus is not really a bus at all in the sense that it is made up of a number of individual lines, each of which has its own specific function. This is different from the data and address buses, where all the lines work together as a unit to code an item of data or an address.

ADDRESSABILITY

Main memory is typically made up of thousands of millions of storage locations which are **addressable** by the processor. Each location is identified by a unique address.

Calculation of Main Memory Capacity

A processor with a 32-bit address bus and a 24-bit data bus can create $2^{32} = 4\,294\,967\,296$ addresses. There are 2^{32} addressable memory locations, and each holds 24 bits.
The maximum memory size that this processor can support is $2^{32} \times 24$ bits $= 2^{32} \times 3$ bytes $= 12$ Gb.

(A computer might not be supplied with 12 Gb of memory for reasons such as the cost of memory, or because current applications normally don't need that much.)

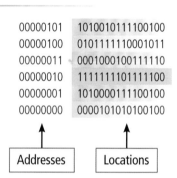

Addresses	Locations
00000101	1010010111100100
00000100	0101111110001011
00000011	0001000100111110
00000010	1111111101111100
00000001	1010000111100100
00000000	0000101010100100

MEMORY READ AND WRITE OPERATIONS

During the execution of a program, the processor reads data from memory locations and writes data to memory locations.

Memory Read

A processor reads instructions from memory as part of the **fetch–execute cycle** or reads items of data to perform a calculation.
Step 1 The processor sets up the address bus with the address of the required memory location.
Step 2 The processor activates the READ line on the control bus.
Step 3 The contents of the memory location are transferred along the data bus into the processor.
Step 4 If it is an instruction, it is decoded and executed.

Memory Write

The processor sometimes writes the results of calculations to memory.
Step 1 The processor sets up the address bus with the address of the required memory location.
Step 2 The processor sets up the data bus with the data to be written to memory.
Step 3 The processor activates the WRITE line on the control bus.
Step 4 The data is transferred along the data bus to the memory location.

LET'S THINK ABOUT THIS

There are only a few calculation questions that are required for the Higher course. Even if you are not a strong mathematician, you can still learn the methods. The description of the steps in the fetch–execute cycle requires a description of the role of the three processor buses. Get into the habit of looking at computer adverts in magazines and newspapers to investigate the specification of current computer systems.

SYSTEM PERFORMANCE

MEASURES OF SYSTEM PERFORMANCE

The measures of system performance shown below can be used to compare different computer systems.

MIPS (millions of instructions per second): this is an indication of the amount of instructions that can be fetched and executed per second. However, since the complexity of instructions varies widely between different systems, it is not always a good measure of processor performance.

FLOPS (floating-point operations per second): the operations carried out on floating-point numbers are similar for different processors. This makes this measure a good comparison of the performance of different processors.

The **clock speed** of a processor is measured in GHz and is the number of clock cycles per second. The clock speed is not a good measure of processor performance, since it does not indicate how many bits are being processed in one clock cycle. Programs called **benchmarks** have been specially created to provide a good test of processor performance.

Application-based tests: application software packages can be used to test the performance of a processor. For example, the time taken to sort a large database can be measured.

DON'T FORGET

Some measures of processor performance give a truer comparison than others, since like is being compared with like.

IMPROVING SYSTEM PERFORMANCE

The table below illustrates the trend in improvement in system performance for desktop computers over the past 30 years. The factors listed below have contributed to this improvement.

Factor	1978	2008
Clock speed	2 MHz	3 GHz
Data bus width	8 bits	32 bits
Address bus width	16 bits	32 bits
Main memory	64 Kb	3 Gb
Hard disc	4 Mb	300 Gb

Increasing the Clock Speed

Increasing the clock speed clearly improves processor performance, since more memory reads or writes take place per second. The clock speed in desktop computers has increased considerably from 1 or 2 MHz in the 1970s to a typical clock speed of 4 GHz today.

Width of the Data Bus

Increasing the width of the data bus means that more bits are transferred between the processor and memory in a read or write operation. The data bus width in desktop computers has increased from typically 8 bits in early computers to 32 bits today.

Width of the Address Bus

Increasing the width of the address bus increases the capacity of memory that can potentially be addressed by the processor. This can improve system performance, since large programs and data can be entirely loaded into main memory and not loaded from backing store as the program is being executed, which results in faster processing.

Cache

This is an area of fast-access memory either between the processor and main memory or on the processor chip itself. The **cache** holds instructions and data that are used most frequently. Being in fast-access storage, this increases the overall performance of the system.

Look at the website www.intel.com to investigate the technology of processor chips.

BUFFERS AND SPOOLERS

The processor is much faster at processing data than peripheral devices such as printers and scanners. Buffering and spooling are two techniques used to cope with these differences.

Buffering

A buffer is an area of memory in the device interface used to store data temporarily until the slower device is ready to accept it. Devices such as laser printers can have a large buffer with a capacity of several megabytes.

Spooling

This is the technique of writing a file to be printed to a fast-access backing store device (usually a hard disc) and so freeing the processor to continue with its next task. The file is then sent to the printer from the backing store device for printing at a speed at which the printer can accept it.

DON'T FORGET

On a network, where there can be a large volume of files to be printed, spooling is preferred to buffering since a queue of print requests can be stored on a high-capacity hard disc until the printer is ready to accept them. A buffer is an area of memory which is limited in size and would not be so suited to this situation.

INTERFACE

An **interface** is a combination of the hardware and software between the processor and a device to allow for their differences in speed and operation. The functions of an interface are as follows:

Physical Connection

Typically this will be a wired connection; but wireless connections are becoming more frequent.

Data Format Conversion

The CPU stores data in a different format from the peripheral device. For example, the voltage levels representing 1 and 0 can vary, and analogue-to-digital conversion may be required. It is the function of the interface to perform these conversions.

Data Storage

The interface provides an area to store data until the slower peripheral device is ready to accept it.

Status Information

The interface provides information on the current state of the device. For example, a printer interface will provide information such as: ready to accept more data, out of paper and so on.

Protocol Conversion

A protocol is a set of rules agreed between a sender and receiver so that they can successfully communicate with each other. The interface may require to convert protocols.

PARALLEL AND SERIAL INTERFACES

Serial Interface

In a serial interface, each bit of data is transferred one bit after another down a single line.

Parallel Interface

In a parallel interface, multiple bits are transferred down parallel lines at the same time. Parallel data transmission is clearly faster than serial data transmission.

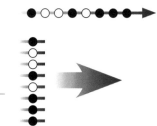

LET'S THINK ABOUT THIS

Increasing the clock speed, the width of the data bus, the width of the address bus, processor cache and improved interfaces have all improved the performance of computer systems. The trend has been for increased processor speed, larger-capacity main memory and backing storage and faster-transmission data transfers between the CPU and peripheral devices.

NETWORKING 1

LANS, WANS, INTRANET, INTERNET

Local-area network

A **LAN** connects computers over a building or site by cables or wireless connections. Each computer on a LAN is called a station.

Wide-area network

A **WAN** connects computers over large distances, such as different towns or countries. The computers in a WAN are usually joined using telecommunications and include satellite links, microwave transmission and optical fibres.

An **intranet** is the implementation of the internet on a private network. For example, a school may have an intranet to provide web pages on courses and events.

The **internet** is a global network of interconnected computer networks and individual computers.

DON'T FORGET

A mainframe-and-terminals system is not considered to be a network since, unlike a network, the dumb terminals have no processing power and memory of their own.

MAINFRAMES AND NETWORKS

Before the growth of computer networks, most organisations had a very expensive and powerful computer called a **mainframe**. Terminals were connected to the mainframe computer, which shared its processing power with many terminals. The terminals had no processing power, memory or backing store of their own.

Most modern organisations use a computer **network** to implement their IT requirements. In a network, the individual workstation computers have their own processor, main memory and backing store. The computers are connected up in a network so that they can share access to files and share resources such as printers.

CLIENT/SERVER AND PEER TO PEER

LANs can be classified as client/server or peer-to-peer networks.

Client/Server

This is a network where there are two levels of computers: servers and clients.

The servers provide a network resource. Most **client/server** networks will have a file server, which stores and manages access to files and data, and a print server, which manages printing on the network by storing a queue of files to be printed.

Other types of servers commonly found on this type of network are a web server, which retrieves and delivers requested web pages to users, and a multimedia server. The clients are the network user's workstations that make use of the resources provided by the servers.

Benefits

There is good security. Different levels of access rights can be provided to users, who log on with a username and password.

Software only has to be installed once on the file server and then made available to the clients.

All software and data is stored centrally on the file server, so it is easy to make backups.

Peer to Peer

In a peer-to-peer network, there are no powerful servers but simply a situation where a small number of computers of equal status are connected together to share resources such as printers and to access the files on each other's hard discs.

contd

CLIENT/SERVER AND PEER TO PEER contd

Limitations

This type of network is best suited to a home or a small office with, at most, eight computers. Above this number of computers, a client/server would be more suited. This is a trusted environment in which there is little security.

Backing up data is difficult, since the data is not saved centrally on a file server. Each computer must be backed up separately.

All software has to be installed separately on each individual computer.

NETWORK INTERFACE CARD (NIC)

A NIC is a circuit board installed in a computer so that it can be connected to a network.

It contains a MAC (Media Access Controller) address which identifies the computer. The MAC address is a 6-byte (48-bit) number. This allows for 2^{48} addresses (approximately 280 billion billion). Every NIC has a unique MAC address.

The data to be transmitted is split up into blocks of data called packets. The packets contain the destination MAC address, the source MAC address, error detection and transmission information along with the data.

The NIC also converts data from the computer into a form that can be broadcast on the network.

REPEATER, HUB, SWITCH AND ROUTER

Data is transmitted around computer networks in groups of bytes called packets. The following are devices used on networks to deliver packets to the correct destination computer.

Repeater

When data is transmitted down a transmission medium, the signal will gradually decay over distance. At a certain point, it is necessary to boost the signal.

A repeater is used to boost and forward packets down a single transmission channel.

Hub

Sometimes it is necessary to branch a transmission channel down two or more channels.

A hub is a multi-port repeater. It boosts and forwards packets down multiple transmission channels.

Switch

A switch is an intelligent hub in the sense that it looks at the address of a packet, amplifies the signal and forwards it down the required channel. A hub blindly broadcasts the packet down all of the channels regardless of the address.

Router

A router is used to route packets between **different** networks. It uses the IP (Internet Protocol) address to route the packets.

DON'T FORGET

It is a common mistake to confuse a switch with a router. A switch routes packets in a LAN, but a router is used to route packets between different networks. For example, the internet uses routers to route packets globally around a large variety of different networks.

LET'S THINK ABOUT THIS

The functions of the network devices Repeater, Hub, Switch and Router are often asked for in the exam. One of the options for Unit 3 in this course, 'Computer Networking', covers computer networks in much more detail than in the compulsory 'Computer Systems' unit.

NETWORKING 2

TOPOLOGY

The **topology** of a network is the position of the computers and how they are interconnected. The computers and devices on a network are often referred to as nodes.

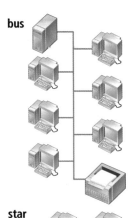

bus

Bus

In a bus topology network, there is a single main cable into which the nodes are connected.

Advantages
It is very easy to expand by connecting a new computer to the main bus.
The failure of a single computer will not affect the rest of the network.

Disadvantages
There is a lot of congestion, since all computers use the same main cable, and data collisions can occur often. If the main channel fails, then the entire network is disabled.

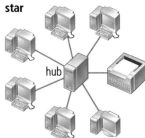

star

Star

In a star topology, all the nodes have their own link to a central computer called a hub.

Advantages
There is a direct path between any computer and the central file server.
It is very easy to expand by adding an extra connection to the hub.
Failure of a channel disables the computer connected to the channel but has no effect on the rest of the network.

Disadvantages
Failure of the central node results in complete failure of the network, although failure of any other computer will not affect the network.
There is the possibility of a high congestion of network traffic at the central node.

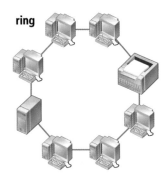

ring

Ring

In a ring topology, all the nodes are connected together in a circle.

Advantages
If a single computer fails, then the rest of the network remains operational since there is a mechanism for the channel to bypass the computer.
There are few data collisions, because a control system is in charge of data transmissions.

Disadvantages
Channel failure results in entire failure of the complete network.
To expand the network, it requires the network to be shut down while the extra node is inserted into the ring.

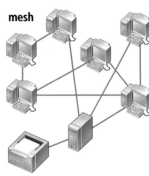

mesh

Mesh

This topology is a subset of a fully distributed topology in that some but not all of the possible connections are made.

Advantages
The network is still operational in case of a channel failure, since there is a choice of routes between the sender and the receiver.
A node failure will not affect the operation of the rest of the network.

Disadvantages
The cost of cabling can be high, especially if using expensive cabling such as optical fibres.

DON'T FORGET

There are other network topologies, but these are the ones that you should be able to describe and give their advantages and disadvantages.

Explore network topologies further by entering the keywords 'Wikipedia' and 'Topology' into a search engine.

TRANSMISSION MEDIA

Criteria that can be used to evaluate transmission media are bandwidth, maximum distance and security. The speed of a transmission medium is referred to as its bandwidth, usually measured in bits per second. The maximum distance is the furthest distance recommended before which the signal will begin to deteriorate significantly.

Electrical cables are not very secure, since the electrical field can be tapped. Optical fibres transmit the data as light and are much more secure. Wireless transmissions are not secure, since they can be captured by any receiver.

The table below shows transmission media commonly used on networks.

Medium	Maximum Distance	Typical Bandwidth	Security
Co-axial cable	300 metres	10 Mb/sec	Poor
UTP (Unshielded Twisted Pair)	100 metres	100 Mb/sec	Poor
Optical fibre	1000 metres	1000 Mb/sec	Very good
Microwave	Line of sight	Very high speed	Very poor

DON'T FORGET

It is a common mistake to confuse units of capacity such as kilobytes and megabytes with bandwidth units such as Kbps and Mbps.
10 megabytes =
10 × 1 048 576 bytes, whereas 10 Mbps =
10 × 1 048 576 bits per second.
NB: Bandwidth is expressed in **bits**, not **bytes**.

TECHNICAL REASONS FOR GROWTH OF NETWORKS

Transmission Media: Faster and more reliable transmission media are now available such as optical fibres, and there is an increase in the use of wireless connections.

Standard Protocols: The internet uses a standard **protocol** called TCP/IP which allows dissimilar networks to communicate with each other.

Improved Hardware: Faster processors, higher-capacity main memory and backing stores have improved the performance of computer networks and therefore made them a more attractive proposition to organisations.

LEGAL ACTS

Data Protection Act: This act is concerned with individuals' rights in society that their confidential information held on computer systems is used correctly. It states that the data should be made secure, people have a right to see what data is being stored about them (except for the police database), incorrect data must be corrected, data no longer required should be deleted, and other measures.

Computer Misuse Act: This act is concerned with hacking into confidential data on computer systems and sending destructive viruses.

Copyright, Design and Patents Act: This act makes it illegal to breach copyright concerned with music, literature and so on.

DON'T FORGET

The majority of questions in this course are to do with technical issues; but remember that social issues such as these three laws also play a significant part.

LET'S THINK ABOUT THIS

Answers to questions on network topologies can be enhanced with a labelled diagram of the topologies. Bandwidth, distance and security should all be considered when choosing a transmission medium for a network.

COMPUTER SOFTWARE 1

OPERATING SYSTEM

An **operating system** is a large program which manages the hardware and software of the computer system. Windows Vista and Mac OS are examples of operating systems.

ROM or Disc

Early computers had their operating system stored in ROM, which meant that the program could be run as soon as the power was switched on.

Modern computers have their operating system stored on the hard disc, which means that there is a delay while it is loaded from the backing store into RAM. The main advantage of this is that it makes it much easier to upgrade the operating system. However, disc-based operating systems can be corrupted by other programs, but operating systems stored in ROM cannot be overwritten.

Bootstrap Loader

When the computer is switched on, a small program called the bootstrap loader program is run which locates the operating system on the hard disc and loads it into main memory.

FIVE COMPONENTS OF AN OPERATING SYSTEM

The **operating system** can be described in terms of five components.

1 Command-Language Interpreter

The command-language interpreter component provides the interface to allow the user to communicate commands to the operating system. It takes input from the user, such as dragging a file into the bin, and passes it to the part of the operating system that implements it. (In this case, the file-management component of the operating system would update the directory on the disc to delete the file.)

2 File Management

The file-management component manages the files saved on disc and deleted from disc by keeping directories containing details of files such as their filename and their address on the disc. The system also keeps tables describing the hierarchical directory structure created by the user.

Shown below is a hierarchical directory structure where a root directory contains subdirectories which themselves can contain files or further subdirectories.

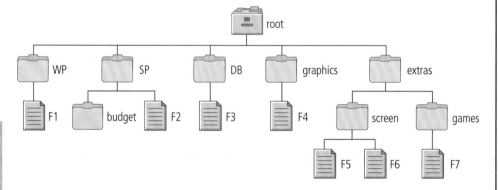

3 Memory Management

This component of the operating system allocates programs and data files to the space available in main memory. It manages the placement of programs and data files so that they do not overwrite each other.

DON'T FORGET

The file management system manages files held on backing store, but the memory management system manages files held in main memory.

contd

FIVE COMPONENTS OF AN OPERATING SYSTEM contd

4 Input/Output

The input/output component of the operating system is responsible for performing data transfers between the CPU and peripheral devices such as keyboards and printers. The software may already be part of the operating system or may have to be installed. For example, when a new printer is bought, it will come with software called a printer driver which can be installed from disc.

5 Process Management (Kernel)

At any given time, the processor can be managing the execution of two or more programs. For example, the user might be entering text into a word-processing document in the foreground while printing is taking place in the background. The operating system has to share the processor's time between these two processes.

Resource Allocation

Resource allocation describes the process of allocating the available hardware of the computer system to tasks generated by running programs. For example, a system with a dual processor requires the operating system to allocate each processor to the execution of one particular program. Another example would be where the operating system has to allocate the printing of a document to one of several available printers.

UTILITY PROGRAMS

A **utility program** is a program used to look after and maintain the computer system.

Disc repair: This utility is used to recover files from corrupted discs and in some cases can recover deleted files.

Defragmenter: When files are continually being written to a disc and deleted from it, the parts of a file can become scattered throughout the surface of the disc. This can considerably slow down the loading of a file, since the read/write head on the disc must move around the disc. A defragmenter utility reads in the files to main memory and then rewrites them to the disc so that the scattered fragments are reunited on the disc.

File compression: This utility is used to reduce the size of a file and can be used to free up more room on backing store devices.

Anti-virus: This utility checks the system for the presence of viruses by looking for suspicious activity. For example, the anti-virus software can look for the sudden increased size of a program file or a set of instructions that is recognised to be the signature of a known virus.

DON'T FORGET

Anti-virus software must be updated regularly, since new viruses are being produced all the time.

STANDARD FILE FORMAT FOR GRAPHICS

Standard file formats have been created to allow data to be recognised by different software applications. For example, a file created in the graphics application Photoshop could be opened by other graphics programs if it was saved in a standard file format for graphics such as GIF, JPEG or TIFF.

JPEG (Joint Photographic Expert Group) is a standard file format that compresses the file by grouping colours of a similar shade into the same colour. This is called **'lossy' compression**, since some of the detail is lost in the compressed file.

GIF (Graphics Interchange Format) uses a compression algorithm that looks for particular bit patterns. This is an example of **lossless compression**, since none of the detail of the original is lost.

Use the internet to look up other standard file formats for graphics such as TIFF.

LET'S THINK ABOUT THIS

Operating systems are large programs. Find out how much memory the operating system takes up on the hard disc on your computer. There are many other operating systems apart from Windows and Mac OS. Research other operating systems.

COMPUTER SOFTWARE 2

DON'T FORGET

'Virtual memory' is the process of loading parts of a program from the hard disc as the program is being run. The program will run more slowly than if the entire program could be loaded into RAM.

SOFTWARE COMPATIBILITY

A program will not run on a particular computer system unless it is compatible with the hardware and the software environment. The main factors that affect compatibility are the size of RAM, hard-disc capacity and the operating system.

RAM

Software applications will specify a minimum amount of RAM required to run the software. Very often, a program will run with the minimum of RAM but will run slowly, as parts of the program have to be loaded from the hard disc when required, and this takes time.

Hard Disc

Manufacturers specify a minimum hard-disc capacity to run their programs. Obviously, there must be sufficient capacity not only to store the program itself but also to store the system's operating system and data files. In some application areas, such as video editing and graphics, the data files can be very large.

Operating System

A program written to run on a Windows Vista operating system will not run on a Mac OS operating system. Operating systems are constantly being upgraded, so the version of the operating system being used will also be a factor.

VIRUSES, WORMS AND TROJAN HORSES

Virus

A virus is a program that causes harm to a computer system. It can also replicate itself and spread to other computers.

Worm

The main aim of a **worm** is to propagate itself. This can use up the resources of a system to the point that it grinds to a halt.

Trojan Horse

A Trojan horse is a program that allows an intruder to gain access to the computer system that it has infected.

TYPES OF VIRUS

There are **three** main types of virus.

File Virus

A file virus infects the system by attaching itself to a program file. The next time the program is loaded into memory, the virus is loaded too and carries out its action.

Macro Virus

A macro virus is a misuse of an applications programming language which is normally used to write macros. These languages are provided to allow a program to be customised by the user, but the same language can be used to write a virus that performs destructive actions.

contd

TYPES OF VIRUS contd

Boot-Sector Virus

The boot sector of a disc contains system data that is used by the operating system. The boot-sector virus writes itself to the boot sector and is activated the next time the bootstrap loader program is run.

VIRUS CODE ACTIONS

Replication

This is the process of the virus propagating itself. Often, a virus will replicate itself many times before it becomes active, thus increasing the havoc that it causes.

Camouflage

Viruses can camouflage themselves against detection by anti-virus software by using groups of instructions that anti-virus software is programmed to take as being harmless.

Watching

Viruses can lie dormant until activated by a particular date, a sequence of actions performed by the user and so on.

Delivery

The most common way for viruses to infiltrate a computer system is through e-mails. A lot of companies forbid their employees from opening e-mail attachments, which often contain viruses.

ANTI-VIRUS DETECTION TECHNIQUES

Searching for Virus Signature

Viruses can be identified by looking for a series of bits that is characteristic of known viruses.

Checksum

When a program is first installed, a checksum calculation is performed on the program data. This checksum can be recalculated every time the program is run, and a change in its value could indicate that a virus has attached itself to the program file.

Memory-Resident Monitoring

Some anti-virus programs are loaded into main memory when the computer is switched on. The software remains there and continually checks the system for viruses. The trade-off is that the time taken to perform the checks can cause delays.

Heuristic Detection

This detection works on the principle that one example of suspicious activity might not be strong evidence for the existence of a virus but that several can add up to a high probability of a virus being present. For example, if a program accesses an e-mail address book and then writes to the disc boot sector, then the possibility of a virus being present increases.

DON'T FORGET

A checksum is performed by treating the program bytes as numbers and calculating the total of all the bytes. Some of the digits of this sum can then be used as a checksum. Any change to this checksum would indicate that the program has changed.

Look at the website www.norton-online.com to find out more about anti-virus software.

LET'S THINK ABOUT THIS

The compatibility of a software package with a computer system depends on the amount of RAM, hard-disc capacity and the operating system.

Replication, Camouflage, Watching and Delivery are actions performed by viruses.

HARDWARE – INPUT DEVICES

DON'T FORGET

It is a common mistake to state that backing store devices are input devices or output devices. Of course, a backing store device such as a hard disc drive performs input and output operations as it loads and saves files, but it is classified as a backing store device since it permanently stores data.

DON'T FORGET

Accuracy, capacity, speed and cost are the only characteristics of peripheral devices that matter for this course. Other characteristics such as the bulkiness of a printer or even its colour may well be a factor when selecting one, but stick to the requirements when answering exam questions on characteristics of devices.

DON'T FORGET

The accuracy of a scanner is how closely the data being input represents the original image. The more colours that can be represented (more bit depth) and the smaller the pixels (high resolution), then the closer the scanned image is to the original.

INTRODUCTION

A computer system is made up of a CPU and peripheral devices that are attached to the CPU. The peripheral devices are classified as input, output and backing store devices.

CHARACTERISTICS OF HARDWARE DEVICES

Accuracy	How close the data input or output is to the original. Accuracy is concerned with the resolution, bit depth and sampling of a peripheral device.
Capacity	The amount of data that can be stored on a device – for example, the amount of data that can be stored on a hard disc.
Speed	How fast data can be transferred between the computer and a peripheral device.
Cost	Self-evident!

INPUT DEVICES

Keyboard

Accuracy
The key that the user types must always be the key that appears on the display, so that a keyboard must be 100 per cent accurate.

Capacity
Keyboards do not store large amounts of data. However, a small number of characters will be stored in the buffer in the interface until the processor is ready to input them into main memory.

Speed
The speed of data transfer of a keyboard is clearly dependent on how fast the user can type. A good typist can type around 75 words per minute.

Cost
Keyboards cost between £10 and £30.

Scanner

Accuracy
This is determined by the bit depth and the **resolution** (dpi). Typically, a mid-range scanner will have a resolution of around 2400 dpi and 24-bit depth.

Capacity
The capacity of the scanner is not relevant here, since the data is transferred directly into the main memory of the computer when an image is scanned.

Speed
The speed will depend more on the speed at which the computer can transfer the data from the scanner to the computer than on the scanner. The type of interface (USB, parallel, SCSI and so on) will have an influence on the speed of data transfer.

Cost
A basic scanner will cost around £40. This can rise to many £1000s for the high-resolution and high-bit-depth scanners used in the production of commercial magazines and so on.

Digital Camera

Accuracy
This is influenced by the number of megapixels and the bit depth. Typically, a modern digital camera would support around 10 megapixels.

contd

INPUT DEVICES contd

Capacity
A digital camera has a memory card to store the images. The capacity of the cards can range from around 128 Mb to several Gb.

Speed
The speed at which images are downloaded to the computer is dependent on the computer itself and on the type of interface being used.

Cost
Digital cameras can vary from £40 to many £1000s depending on the specification of the device.

Sound Card

Sampling frequency
This is the number of times per second that the sound is sampled. For example, if the sampling frequency is 48 Khz, then the sampler listens 48 000 times a second and stores a description of the sound in binary numbers each time.

Sampling depth
The number of bits used to store each sample is called the sampling depth. The two most common sampling depths are 16-bit and 24-bit. A higher sampling depth represents the sound with greater definition.

Accuracy
How closely the digitised sound matches the original will clearly depend upon the sampling frequency and sampling depth.

Capacity
The capacity of the sound card is not relevant here, since the data is transferred directly to the computer.

Speed
The speed at which the data is transferred is dependent on the computer system itself.

Cost
The price of a sound card varies from around £10 for a basic sound card to well over £100.

Video-Capture Cards

A video-capture card converts a video signal into a form that can be input into a computer by digitising the video in a number of frames per second.

Accuracy
Accuracy is determined by the resolution, the bit depth and the number of frames captured per second.

Capacity
The video data is stored on the hard disc of the computer itself.

Speed
Speed is measured by the number of frames that are captured by the card per second. Typically, a video-capture card will support up to 30 frames per second.

Cost
Prices range from around £50 to a few hundred pounds.

Look at the website www.pcworld. co.uk to explore the characteristics of input devices and keep up to date with their prices.

LET'S THINK ABOUT THIS

There are many more input devices other than the ones listed in this book. However, the ones described are frequently asked for in the exam, so learn their characteristics of accuracy, capacity and speed, and have an idea of their cost.

In the coursework task, you will be given a real-life scenario and a budget and then given the task of selecting actual devices for the implementation of a computing system.

HARDWARE – OUTPUT DEVICES

INTRODUCTION

The same characteristics of accuracy, capacity, speed and cost which were used to evaluate input devices can be used to evaluate output devices.

OUTPUT DEVICES

Inkjet Printers

These printers are widely used in homes, where the best speed and quality is not too important and the cost is relatively low. However, ink cartridges for these printers can run out quickly and are expensive (typically around £15 per cartridge).

Accuracy
This is a measure of the resolution and bit depth of the printer.

Typically, an inkjet printer would have a resolution of 2400 dpi and true colour.

Capacity
A buffer in the printer's interface stores data until the printer is ready to accept it.

Speed
The speed of a printer is measured in pages per minute (ppm). The speed of inkjet printers can be as high as 15 ppm for monochrome printing but slower in colour.

Cost
The price starts from around £40 but rises to a few hundred pounds for the best-quality inkjet printers.

Laser Printers

These printers are used mainly in business and on networks, where often quality and speed are the main consideration. Laser printers use a toner to produce the printout rather than ink cartridges. Toner cartridges cost between £50 and £200 but produce many more pages than an ink cartridge.

The price of these printers has dropped from many thousands of pounds to a few hundred, which is now making them a viable option for the home user.

Accuracy
This is influenced by the resolution and bit depth of the printer.

Typically, a laser printer can provide resolutions of 2400 dpi. The best inkjet printers can offer much the same resolution, but the laser operates at a much faster speed.

Capacity
The better-quality laser printers can store a large amount of data until the printer is ready to accept it.

Typically, a laser printer would have around 64 Mb of memory.

Speed
Laser printers can print at speeds of 32 ppm in monochrome. Speeds for laser printers are faster than for inkjet printers.

Cost
Prices start at a few hundred pounds but rise to many thousands for top-end colour laser printers.

contd

OUTPUT DEVICES contd

Multiscan Monitors

Most multiscan monitors use a cathode ray tube (CRT) to produce the image by mixing different amounts of red, green and blue to make different colours on a phosphorescent screen.

The image on the screen is redrawn many times per second. To avoid flickering, the screen has to be refreshed at least 50 times per second.

Common sizes of multiscan monitors are 17-inch and 21-inch.

Accuracy
The resolution is described by the **dot pitch** instead of the dots per inch which are used to describe the resolution of most other devices. Dot pitch is the distance between two adjacent dots on the screen. This ranges between 0.28 mm and 0.38 mm. These values correspond to between 70 and 100 dots per inch (dpi).

The number of colours that can be represented will depend upon the bit depth.

Speed
The number of times that the screen is refreshed per second is called the scan rate or refresh rate. Scan rates start at around 50 Hz and go up to 85 Hz.

Cost
The price of a basic multiscan monitor is around £100 but goes up to several hundred pounds for a high-resolution good-quality monitor.

Flat Screens

Flat screens have the advantage of being much lighter and less bulky than multiscan monitors. They are therefore ideal for portable devices such as laptop and palmtop computers. In the last few years, their smaller size has meant that they have virtually taken over as the display for desktop computers.

LCD (Liquid Crystal Display)
This is a flat-screen display that produces the image by applying a voltage to crystals that change colour when electricity is applied. LCD displays use up much less power than CRT monitors.

TFT Monitors (Thin Film Transistor)
This display produces the image by controlling the state of each pixel with a tiny resistor.

The prices of flat-screen monitors range from around £100 to several hundred pounds.

 Look at the website www.pcworld.co.uk to explore the characteristics of output devices and keep up to date with their prices.

LET'S THINK ABOUT THIS

Research other output devices such as sound cards for outputting audio and computer output on microfilm (COM).

The characteristics of accuracy, capacity, speed and cost should be considered when selecting a peripheral device to operate in a real-life situation.

HARDWARE – STORAGE DEVICES

DON'T FORGET

When accessing data from a disc, the data can be read randomly from any part of the disc. This type of access is called direct or random access. However, reading data from a tape requires winding through other data on the tape to get to the required data. This type of access is called **sequential access**. The type of access is important when considering a storage device. Direct access is faster at accessing data than sequential access.

INTRODUCTION

Backing store devices can be classified as magnetic, optical or solid-state devices.

Magnetic devices store bits in two states of magnetisation on a specially coated surface. They include hard disc, floppy disc and magnetic tape.

Optical devices use a laser to read and write data in the form of pits and lands on the surface of a disc. They include CDs and DVDs.

Solid-state storage devices have no moving parts but are made entirely of electronic components. They include memory cards (flash cards) used in digital cameras and USB memory sticks.

Accuracy of Storage Devices

The storing and retrieving of data on and from a storage device has to be 100 per cent accurate and so will not be discussed as a characteristic of storage devices.

STORAGE DEVICES

Hard Disc Drive

Capacity
A typical hard disc on a desktop computer has a capacity of between 100 and 200 gigabytes.

Speed
The speed of access to data on a disc is given by the formula:

Access time = Seek time + Latency time + Read/Write time.

The seek time is the time taken for the read/write head to move over the correct track on the disc. The latency time is the time taken for the disc to rotate to the correct sector on the disc, which will depend partly on the rotational speed of the hard disc (typically around 7200 rpm). The read/write time is the actual time required to read or write the data. The speed of data transfer will also depend on the type of interface being used. Transfer rates of 60 Mb per second are typical.

Access
A hard disc drive is a **direct-access** device.

Cost
A hard disc drive can cost from around £30 to a few hundred pounds.

Floppy Disc Drive

Capacity
A floppy disc has a capacity of 1.44 megabytes, has a slower data-transfer rate than a hard disc, is a direct-access device and costs about 10p.

Magnetic Tape

Capacity
Magnetic tapes have capacities which can be as large as several gigabytes.

Speed
The speed of data transfer can go up to as high as 4.8 Mb per second.

Access
Magnetic tape has sequential access to data.

DON'T FORGET

Floppy discs have been disappearing as storage devices for computer systems since the appearance of much higher-capacity and more portable devices such as USB memory sticks. However, you should still know the characteristics of floppy discs for the purposes of this course. You may well be asked: 'Why is a floppy disc **not** suitable in this situation?'

contd

STORAGE DEVICES contd

Cost
Magnetic tape drives can **cost** from £100 to well over £1000, but the tapes themselves are cheap and cost only a few pounds.

CD-ROM (Compact Disc Read-Only Memory)

CD-ROM discs can only be used to read data stored on them – the user cannot save data to the disc.

Capacity
CD-ROMs are typically 650 Mb in capacity.

Speed
In a single-speed CD reader, data can be read at a rate of 150 Kb/sec.
A multiple-speed CD reader such as 48× reads data at a rate of 48 × 150 Kb/sec = 7.2 Mb/sec.

Access
CD-ROM access is direct.

Cost
CD drives cost in the range of £30 to a few hundred pounds, but the discs themselves are cheap and cost around 40p.

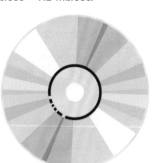

CD-R (CD-Recordable)
The CD-R drive uses a laser to burn data onto the surface of the disc.
CD-Rs can be written to only once.

CD-RW (Recordable/Writeable)
This type of CD can not only record data but also erase current data and store new data.
Three numbers are used to indicate record speed, rewrite speed and read speed: for example, 24 × 16 × 48.

DVD (Digital Versatile Disc)

These are very high-capacity discs and are suited to acting as a storage device for large amounts of data such as full-length movies.

Capacity
The capacity of DVD discs goes up to 17 Gb.

Speed
At present, 16× DVD Write, 8× Rewrite and 16× Read are typical speeds.

Cost
DVD drives and discs were at one time much more expensive than CD drives and discs, but the price has now fallen to a similar level.

Solid-State Storage Devices (SSSD)

Capacity
Memory sticks and memory cards typically have a capacity in the range of 128 Mb to 16 Gb.

Speed
Memory cards and memory sticks can operate read and write speeds of hundreds of megabits per second.

Cost
The cost can vary from a few pounds to around £100.

 LET'S THINK ABOUT THIS

The portability of a storage device can sometimes be important when choosing a suitable storage device. For example, when distributing data to thousands of clients, a CD is appropriate but a hard disc is not! In general, the price of computer hardware is improving in performance as the price is falling. It is important to keep up with current prices and specifications of storage devices through the internet and computing literature.

TYPICAL TASKS

INTRODUCTION

This topic brings together the knowledge developed about computer systems into a real-life situation where you are asked to select appropriate hardware and software to support a typical task. This involves selecting a computer system, input, output and backing store devices and application and system software.

The characteristics of the components have to be considered in the context of the task. For example, the printer selected for the production of a colour catalogue requires to have a high resolution, bit depth and speed to quickly produce the quality graphics required for a colour magazine. The performance of the CPU is also important. The main factors to be considered are the processor speed, the amount of RAM and the hard-disc capacity.

The course requires you to select and justify your choice of hardware and software to support the following three tasks:

1 Production of a multimedia catalogue

2 Setting up a school LAN

3 Development of a school website.

PRODUCTION OF A MULTIMEDIA CATALOGUE

Hardware Requirements

A computer with a 4 **GHz** processor, 2 gigabytes of RAM, 200 Gb hard disc and good-quality video and sound cards.

This is a high-specification computer system since it needs a fast processor and a large amount of main memory to load up and edit graphics, video and sound files.

Peripherals
- A digital camera to capture images. It should have a high-capacity memory card and a high number of megapixels and bit depth to capture accurate images.

- A digital video camera to capture video.

- A microphone and good-quality sound card to capture sound.

- CD-RW and DVD-RW drives to store the large multimedia files in a portable and cheap format so that they can be distributed easily to clients.

Software Requirements

An operating system, for example Windows Vista.

A multimedia authoring package, which is software used to produce a stand-alone multimedia program.

SETTING UP A SCHOOL LAN

Hardware Requirements

- A file server and a print server. These computers require to have a fast processor to deal with the high volume of network traffic; and the file server in particular must have a very high-capacity hard disc to store all the application programs and the network users' data files. Also, a magnetic tape drive would be useful to make regular backups cheaply.

contd

SETTING UP A SCHOOL LAN contd

- 100 network workstations with network interface cards. The workstations would require a reasonably fast processor and a fairly large amount of RAM to run the applications downloaded from the file server. However, they would not require much hard-disc capacity, since allocation and data files are stored permanently on the file server.

- Five laser printers. The printers will require a fairly high speed (ppm) to cope with a high number of print requests from all the network users. The resolution and bit depth would not require to be too high a specification in most situations, since it is not a commercial business.

- Repeaters, hubs and switches to improve the performance of the network by amplifying and routing packets on the network.

- UTP cabling connection operating at 100 Mbps. This is a mid-range bandwidth which would be fine for the volume of network traffic found in a typical school.

Software Requirements

The file server is running a network operating system.
The workstations are running Windows Vista.

DEVELOPMENT OF A SCHOOL WEBSITE

Hardware Requirements

A computer with a 3 GHz processor, 512 megabytes of RAM and 100 **Gb** hard disc.

A fairly high specification is required for the computer system, since web pages can have a high multimedia content (graphics, video, sound), which requires a lot of storage and a fast processor to deal with the large files associated with this type of data.

Peripherals
- A digital camera to capture images for the web pages.

- A digital video camera to capture video.

- A microphone and good-quality sound card to capture sound.

Software Requirements

- An operating system, for example Windows Vista.

- A text editor to create web pages using HTML code.

- A web-page editor, for example FrontPage or Dreamweaver to create web pages more quickly than using HTML code.

A browser to display web pages and navigate between them, for example Internet Explorer.

LET'S THINK ABOUT THIS

The specification of a computer system, the characteristics of the peripheral devices and the operating system and application software all have to be considered when selecting hardware and software to support a task.

It is essential that you know the typical specification of a modern computer system in terms of processor speed (4 GHz), amount of RAM (2 Gb) and hard-disc capacity (200 Gb).

COMPUTER SYSTEMS

EXAM-STYLE QUESTIONS

INTRODUCTION

The following five questions are based on the work of the Computer Systems unit. They are intended to be similar to the level and style of questions that you can expect in the exam. Of course, five questions cannot cover the entire syllabus, and you should make good use of past exam papers for your exam preparation.

QUESTION 1

Standards have been developed for representing numbers, text and graphics in binary on computer systems. Often a compromise is made between the accuracy and range of the data and the storage requirements.

(a) Give **two** reasons why computers use the binary number system and not the decimal number system to store data.

(b) What is the largest whole number that can be stored in 32 bits?

(c) Write down the two's complement 8-bit representation of −39.

(d) ASCII and Unicode are standards for representing text in a computer system. Give one advantage that each standard has over the other.

(e) Explain how the image shown below would be stored in vector graphics.

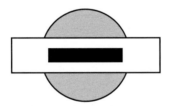

(2, 2, 2, 2, 2)

QUESTION 2

A catalogue is to be produced for a mail-order company that makes garden gnomes. Each of 80 pages will contain six photographs of gnomes. All the pictures will be 2" × 1.5" in 16-bit colour and 600 dpi.

(a) A digital camera is used to take the photographs of the gnomes. How is the accuracy of a digital camera measured?

(b) Calculate the storage requirements of one photograph in megabytes. (Give your answer to one decimal place.)

(c) Suggest a suitable portable storage device that could be used to hold the entire collection of photographs required for the catalogue, and **justify** your answer.

(d) A sample of the photographs has to be sent to the company director as e-mail attachments. Name a utility program that could be used in this situation, and explain why it is useful.

(e) The director is not pleased with the quality of the photographs and asks for the photographs to be retaken in true colour. What effect would this have on the storage requirements for the photographs?

(1, 3, 2, 2, 2)

QUESTION 3

This diagram shows the simplified structure of a desktop computer. C, A and D represent the three processor buses.

Processor

C   A   D

Main memory

C = control bus
A = address bus (32 bits)
D = data bus (32 bits)

(a) Describe the step involved when the processor fetches and executes an instruction held in main memory.
(Your answer should refer to the role of processor buses and registers.)

(b) (i) Calculate the memory capacity that is potentially addressable by this processor.
(ii) Give **two** reasons why all the addressable memory might not be installed.

(c) (i) Which control bus line would be used in the event of a power failure?
(ii) What is the function of the reset line on the control bus?

(4, 4, 2)

QUESTION 4

The Chicago Cab Company has a small office which uses five stand-alone computers to do the company administration. The director is considering networking the computers together to improve the efficiency of the system.

(a) (i) **State** whether a client/server network or a peer-to-peer network is best for this situation, and **justify** your answer.
(ii) Describe **two** disadvantages of a peer-to-peer network compared to a client/server network.

(b) A new printer is to be chosen for the network.
State **one** characteristic, other than cost, that should be considered when buying a printer.

(c) The network will be used mainly to transmit data held in word-processing documents, spreadsheets and databases. Suggest a suitable transmission medium to be used on the network, and give a **reason** for your choice.

(d) The company goes ahead and installs its network using the topology shown here.

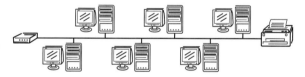

Name this topology, and give one advantage and one disadvantage over a mesh topology.

(4, 1, 2, 3)

QUESTION 5

Mr Semibreve is a music teacher in La Guardia School of Performing Arts in New York. He has paid a software development company to produce a multimedia catalogue to help the students understand the quality of sound of various musical instruments. The software will contain colour pictures and sound for each musical instrument as well as videos that will be used to demonstrate playing techniques.

(a) **Name** a suitable software package that can be used to produce the multimedia catalogue.

(b) List the characteristics (processor speed, RAM, backing store capacity) of a desktop computer that could be used to produce the multimedia catalogue, and **justify** your choice.

(c) (i) Name **three** devices which would be required to capture the picture, sound and video files for the catalogue.
(ii) For each device, describe what is meant by its accuracy.

(1, 3, 6)

ANSWERS

QUESTION 1

2 × 1 mark for each reason

(a) A two-state with 'on' and 'off' is relatively easy to design.
Arithmetic calculations are simpler since there are fewer permutations of 1s and 0s.
Backing store devices can represent two states for 1 and 0 such as two states of magnetisation.

2 marks

(b) $2^{32} - 1 = 4\,294\,967\,295$ since there are 2^{32} different numbers that can be represented in 32 bits. The largest number is 1 less, since the smallest number is 0.

2 marks

(c) The table shows how to find the two's complement of −39.

−128	64	32	16	8	4	2	1	
0	0	1	0	0	1	1	1	39
1	1	0	1	1	0	0	0	Flip 1s and 0s
						+	1	Add 1
1	1	0	1	1	0	0	1	−39

2 marks

(d) ASCII uses less storage than Unicode since each character is coded in 8 bits compared to 16 bits. Unicode can represent 2^{16} characters (65 536) whereas ASCII can only represent 2^7 characters (128).

2 marks

(e) The image is stored as a list of objects (Rectangle, Circle, Line) and their attributes.

QUESTION 2

1 mark

(a) The accuracy is measured in the number of pixels that it can capture, measured in megapixels.

3 marks

(b) The storage requirements of one photograph are $2 \times 1.5 \times 300 \times 300 \times 2$ bytes = 2 160 000 bytes = 2.1 megabytes.

2 marks

(c) The entire collection of photographs requires $80 \times 6 \times 2.1$ Mb = 1008 Mb.
A recordable DVD or a USB stick would have sufficient storage capacity.

2 marks

(d) A file-compression utility could be used to reduce the size of the files and thus allow them to be sent faster as attachments in e-mails.

2 marks

(e) True colour has a bit depth of 24 bits. The increase from 16 bits to 24 bits will increase the storage requirements by a factor of 50 per cent.

QUESTION 3

4 × 1 mark for each step

(a) Step 1 The processor sets up the address bus with the address of the memory location holding the instruction.
Step 2 The processor activates the READ line on the control bus.
Step 3 The instruction is transferred along the data bus into the IR in the processor.
Step 4 The instruction is decoded and executed.

2 marks

(b) (i) The potential amount of memory that can be addressed by this processor is:
$2^{32} \times 4$ bytes = 17 179 869 184 bytes = 16 Gb.

2 × 1 mark for each reason

(ii) Installing 16 Gb of memory would be very expensive.
Most current applications for desktop computers do not require 16 Gb of memory.

1 mark
(c) (i) The non-maskable interrupt line.

1 mark
(ii) The reset line on the control bus clears all processor registers and reboots the computer.

QUESTION 4

(a) (i) A peer-to-peer network is most suitable because it is a small number of computers in a trusted environment and will save on the expense of server computers. — 2 marks

(ii) Backups are difficult since the network data is stored centrally on a file server. There is limited security. — 2 marks

(b) Accuracy (bit depth or resolution) or speed (pages per minute). — 1 mark

(c) Co-axial cable or UTP, since it is cheap and a high bandwidth is not required in this situation. — 2 marks

(d) A bus topology. — 1 mark
Advantage: the bus network is cheap to cable and is easily expandable compared to a bus network. — 1 mark
Disadvantage: if the main cable fails in a bus network, then the entire network is disabled; but a mesh network can find an alternative route for data packets. — 1 mark

QUESTION 5

(a) A multimedia authoring package. — 1 mark

(b) Graphics, video and sound files have a high capacity, therefore the system will require:
A fast processor (4 GHz) to process a large amount of data.
A large amount of RAM (2 Gb) into which to load the graphics, video and sound files when they are being edited.
A high-capacity hard disc (200 Gb) to permanently store all the large files required for the multimedia application. — 3 × 1 mark for each description with a reason

(c) (i) A digital camera, digital camcorder and microphone combined with a good-quality sound card. — 3 × 1 mark for each device

(ii) The accuracy of a digital camera is the number of megapixels that it can capture.
The accuracy of a digital camcorder is its bit depth, resolution and frames per second.
The accuracy of a sound card is its sample size and sample rate. — 3 × 1 mark for each description of accuracy

SOFTWARE DEVELOPMENT PROCESS – INTRODUCTION AND PERSONNEL

INTRODUCTION

The software development process is a series of stages that are carried out to produce a software project to meet the requirements of an initial specification.

The stages are analysis, design, implementation, testing, documentation, evaluation and maintenance.

Each of these stages will be described in more depth later in this book, but it is useful to give a brief outline at this stage to get a better idea of how the stages follow on from each other.

 Research the software development process in more depth by entering 'Wikipedia' and 'software development process' into a search engine.

Analysis

The requirements of the system are identified and clarified in meetings between the developers and the client. At the end of this stage, a legally binding document called the software specification is produced which specifies exactly what the system has to do and is a basis for the next stage of design.

Design

The user interface, the structure and the detailed logic of the software are designed. Structure diagrams and **pseudocode** are used to represent the structure and the detailed logic respectively.

Implementation

A programming language is chosen, and then the program design is converted into the programming language by a team of programmers.

Testing

The program is thoroughly tested to identify and rectify errors. Test data is chosen to systematically and comprehensively test the software.

Documentation

A technical guide and a user guide are produced to support the software system.

Evaluation

The software system is judged against a set of criteria to evaluate its worth.

Maintenance

At some point in the future, the system will have to be modified to adjust to the client's changing needs.

DON'T FORGET

The stages of the software development process and the order in which they occur are key to understanding this topic. Study the brief description of each stage given here and the order in which they take place.

ITERATION

The software development process is iterative.

Iteration is the process of revisiting a stage in the software development process to modify it in the light of experience gained at a later stage in order to get correct results. For example:

- Errors discovered at the testing stage could require the revisiting of the design stage to correct errors in the logic of the program design.

- Revisiting the analysis stage and re-interviewing the client to gather further information to clarify what is required.

> **DON'T FORGET**
>
> The term 'iterative' is also used in the context of programming languages. Iteration is used in this situation to describe the process of repeating a group of instructions in a loop. Don't confuse this with the use of the term 'iterative' in the context of the software development process.

PERSONNEL

Systems Analyst

The systems analyst carries out an analysis of a problem and acts as an intermediary between the client and the software development team. It is important that the analyst has good people and communication skills to understand and extract the needs of the client.

The analyst has to be able to communicate with the client at a non-technical level and at the same time be able to unambiguously communicate formal, technical specifications to the design team.

Project Manager

The boss in charge of the whole project is the project manager, who leads the software development team, supervises the project and is responsible for budgets, schedules and relations with clients.

The manager uses project-management tools and techniques such as constructing project schedules, calling meetings, setting deadlines for the completion of tasks, monitoring the progress of tasks and so on.

Programmer

The programmer usually works as part of a programming team which implements the software design in a programming language.

Programmers will be responsible for the coding, testing, implementation and maintenance of the software. They will probably have experience in several programming languages, although they will probably only know one or two languages very well.

Client

The clients represent the management who require a new or updated system. They will contact a software development company, which provides the people who will create the new system.

The client will have meetings with the software development team where the existing system will be examined in detail and any problems identified.

Independent Test Group

In general, programmers should not test their own programs since they will be biased about exposing errors in their software, and often the testing will be incomplete and allow errors to pass undetected.

A more rigorous approach to testing is to use Independent Test Groups, who are a group of outsiders whose task is to find errors.

LET'S THINK ABOUT THIS

There are seven stages in the software development process:
Analysis, Design, Implementation, Testing, Documentation, Evaluation and Maintenance.

The project manager, systems analyst, programmer and client all have a role in the software development process.

SOFTWARE DEVELOPMENT PROCESS – ANALYSIS

INTRODUCTION

The software development process begins with an analysis of the existing system. It is important that the needs of the client are clearly identified at this stage, otherwise time and money will be wasted at future stages correcting mistakes in a system that does not do what it is supposed to do. In large organisations with a complex system, the analysis stage can take many months to complete.

At one time, the analysis was carried out by programmers, who had very good technical skills but were not necessarily good at extracting the client's needs. Nowadays, this stage is carried out by a systems analyst, who should have good technical skills as well as good communication skills.

PROJECT PROPOSAL

The project proposal (also known as problem definition) is a document created following a preliminary meeting between the client and the systems analyst to discuss the existing system and establish an early rapport with the client in order to understand their needs. The **systems analyst** will advise the client on the benefits of a new system and the likely cost and timescale.

The project proposal is merely a rough outline of the problem and in no way a legally binding document.

After the preliminary meeting and the production of the project proposal, the clients will have a good idea of the cost and timescale for the project and the potential benefits to their business. They are now in a good position to decide if they wish to proceed with a full-scale analysis or back out of the project without having incurred too much expenditure.

DON'T FORGET

The techniques given below are often asked for in the exam – so learn them.

TECHNIQUES USED AT THE ANALYSIS STAGE

The following are techniques used to extract information on the needs of the client.

Interviewing

The client will call meetings with key personnel within the business. Management and workers will be interviewed to get a whole picture of the needs of the clients. This is an opportunity to identify any problems with the existing system and get a clear picture of what needs to be done.

Observation Notes

The day-to-day running of the business can be observed and notes made of what tasks people carry out in their role as part of the system.

contd

TECHNIQUES USED AT THE ANALYSIS STAGE contd

Inspection of Existing Documentation

Existing documents can be inspected to examine how information is being collected and processed to gain an understanding of the needs of the system. Tracking how information changes over a period of time is often useful.

Questionnaires

Where it is not possible to interview staff directly, the indirect method of asking employees to complete a questionnaire can be used.

 Explore the role of a systems analyst further by entering 'Systems Analyst' into a search engine.

SOFTWARE SPECIFICATION

The software specification is a document produced at the end of the analysis stage. It is the result of an examination of the existing system, clearly identifying the needs of the client.

The **software specification** is:

1 A formal document which gives a clear and unambiguous description of exactly what the software has to do in order to meet the needs of the client.

2 A definition of the boundaries (timescale, budget and so on) of the problem. Defining the scope and boundaries of the problem allows the problem to be contained.

3 A document used as the basis for the design stage which follows next. In order to proceed with the design, every precise detail of the software has to be described in this document.

4 A legally binding contract between the developers and the client. If the final product does not meet the requirements as stated in the software specification, then this document can be used by the client in a court of law to support a legal action.

5 A description of the system at a logical level. It does not mention how the problem is to be solved or what hardware and software will be used in the solution to the problem.

DON'T FORGET

The software specification is not the same as the project proposal. The software specification is an unambiguous detailed description of what the software must do that is a legally binding contract between the client and the developers. The project proposal is an initial outline of the problem to allow the client to decide if it is feasible to proceed with the project. The proposal is not legally binding.

LET'S THINK ABOUT THIS

There is some confusion about the term 'Software Specification', which is given different names in other courses. These include 'Requirements Specification' and 'Operational Requirements Document'.

The Advanced Higher Computing course goes into much more detail on the software development stages. Ask your teacher for study materials to extend your knowledge.

SOFTWARE DEVELOPMENT PROCESS – DESIGN

INTRODUCTION

Once the precise software specification has been agreed, the design of the solution can proceed. There are **three** main stages to the design of the software.

1 Design of the user interface
2 Design of the structure of the software
3 Design of the detailed logic of the software.

DESIGN OF THE USER INTERFACE

It does not matter how good the underlying program is if the user interface does not allow the user to communicate effectively with the program. It is therefore very important that the design takes into account the skills and needs of the end users. The dialogue with the user can be performed through a WIMP or **GUI** interface or keyboard commands. A WIMP interface would be preferable for a beginner, but an expert user would prefer keyboard shortcuts that can be performed more quickly.

The design of the interface can be illustrated in drawings of screen layouts with indications of pull-down menus, text sizes and fonts, colours and so on. Here are a few guidelines that can be followed to make the user interface user-friendly:

1 There should be a consistency in the layouts of the menus, colours and text.
2 Warnings should be given before an action with potentially serious consequences is carried out such as deleting a folder and its contents.
3 It should be possible to reverse actions with an UNDO option.
4 There should be feedback on actions performed, such as a progress bar when copying a disc.
5 Commands should be indicated with simple verbs and not large amounts of text.
6 There should be online help available.

> **DON'T FORGET**
>
> A WIMP or GUI (Graphical User Interface) uses a mouse and pointer to select from pull-down menus and icons.

DESIGN OF THE STRUCTURE OF THE SOFTWARE

The structure of the program is the modules which exist and how they communicate with each other.

Stepwise Refinement

This is the process of repeatedly breaking down larger difficult problems step by step into smaller and smaller easier-to-solve ones. It is easier for a human being to solve a series of small problems than a large and difficult problem.

One advantage of this approach is that it also automatically gives a structure to the solution. It also means that, once manageable parts have been identified in a large project, then the analyst can assign individual tasks to different teams of programmers.

Top-Down Design

Stepwise refinement is sometimes called top-down design, for the obvious reason that you start the process at the top, with the problem as a whole, and work downwards in steps of refinement.

Structure Diagram/Structure Chart

A **structure diagram** shows the **hierarchy** of the program components and how they are linked together. It shows the decomposition of the program in a series of steps into smaller and smaller blocks. The representation is hierarchical in that each level relates to the level above.

contd

DESIGN OF THE STRUCTURE OF THE SOFTWARE contd

Different symbols are used in a structure diagram as follows:

A module requiring further refinement

Repetition

Selection

A module requiring no further refinement

For example, a structure diagram represents the calculation of the average of a list of exam marks.

Average mark program

Level 1

Repeat the following until last mark entered

Calculate average

Show results

Level 2

Get and validate mark

Convert mark to percentage

Format results

Display results

> **DON'T FORGET**
>
> A structure diagram is more than a picture of boxes showing the parts of a program. It is a common mistake **not** to describe it as a **hierarchy** where each level is a refinement of the level above.

DESIGN OF THE DETAILED LOGIC OF THE SOFTWARE

Pseudocode is used at the design stage to give the detailed logic of the program code.

It lies somewhere between programming code and natural language.

Level 1
1.   Get mark
2.   Find grade
3.   Display grade

Level 2
1.1   Do
1.2   Get mark from user
1.3   If mark is not between 0 and 100 give error message
1.4   Until mark is between 0 and 100

2.1   Select case mark
2.2   Case mark 70 or more
2.3   grade equals 'A'
2.4   Case mark between 60 and 69
2.5   grade equals 'B'
2.6   Case mark between 50 and 59
2.7   grade equals 'C'
2.8   End select

3.1   Format grade
3.2   Display grade

Three features of pseudocode are:

1 It describes the detailed logic of a program without having to bother about the details of how it is going to be implemented in the chosen programming language.

2 It shows the control constructs of the algorithm, i.e. looping, branching and so on.

3 It shows the stepwise refinement of the problem in levels of decomposition.

> There are many other methods of representing the design of a program apart from structure diagrams and pseudocode. Try to find some others by entering 'software design methodology' into a search engine.

> **DON'T FORGET**
>
> Never use programming keywords in pseudocode – for example: Let Age = Inputbox("How old are you?").
> Use ordinary English to convey the logic of the instruction – for example: Get Age from user, Enter Age and so on.

 ## LET'S THINK ABOUT THIS

The design stage of the software development process addresses the user interface, structure and detailed logic of the software but is not concerned with the actual language in which the solution will be implemented.

Pseudocode should not use specific language keywords but should show the same detailed logic using a more natural form of English.

SOFTWARE DEVELOPMENT PROCESS – IMPLEMENTATION

INTRODUCTION

Once the design stage is complete, the next stage is to translate the design into a programming language. On a large-scale project, this will be done by a team of programmers led by a systems analyst.

The following points are guidelines for good code in the implementation of the solution which will make it quicker to develop the software and easier to perform maintenance activities in the future.

1   The program should be modular (broken down into procedures and functions).

2   Variables should be given meaningful names such as Number1 and Country as opposed to x and y.

3   **Internal commentary** should be used to explain the function of the code throughout the program listing.

4   Procedures and functions should not be too large and complicated.

5   Pre-written modules libraries should be used to save time in writing and testing of code.

CHOOSING A LANGUAGE

Most Scottish schools use Visual Basic to teach programming to students. There are several other languages that are popular at university level in computing courses. Use the internet to research the languages used at Scottish universities.

There is a wide choice of programming languages available. Sometimes a general-purpose package such as a spreadsheet or a database will be suitable for the solution, since they come with an interface already built in and offer a level of programming to extend the functionality of the basic package.

On the other hand, implementing the solution in a programming language allows the solution to be completely customised to suit the user and does not have the limited programming constraints of a general-purpose package.

There are several factors that should be considered when choosing which programming language to use to implement the solution to the problem.

Some of the more important ones are given below:

1   The type of data (numeric, text, graphics, sound and so on) that the language has to support. For example, a scientific program that requires operations on large numbers would require a language that supports floating-point numbers.

2   The arithmetical and logical operations that are required, and whether the language supports these: for example, string operations to create substrings, join strings together and so on.

3   The operating-system environment in which the program will operate. For example, some programming languages produce compiled programs that operate in a Windows environment.

4   The type of application that is being developed. For example, a multimedia authoring package would be chosen to develop a multimedia application, and a declarative language would be chosen to develop an expert system.

DON'T FORGET

Programming languages are very different in the types of data that they support and the operations on the data that they provide. Some languages are designed for specific purposes such as artificial intelligence or scientific areas, while others are general-purpose and can be used in a wide variety of applications.

contd

CHOOSING A LANGUAGE contd

5 If the speed of execution of the software is important, then a language needs to be chosen that gives a solution with a fast response time.

6 The skills of the programming team must be considered, since there is little point in implementing the solution in a language of which the programmers have no experience.

DON'T FORGET

One or two of the terms used to describe a program are usually asked for in the Knowledge and Understanding component of the exam. To be sure of gaining full marks, learn the precise definitions given here, and don't steer too far away from them. For example, to explain the term 'correct' by saying that 'The program is free from errors' will gain no marks.

TERMS USED TO DESCRIBE A PROGRAM

The following terms can be used to evaluate a piece of software:

Correct

A program is correct if it meets the software specification.

Fit for Purpose

The program solves the problem that it is supposed to solve, i.e. it is correct.

Readable

The program code is easily understood by another programmer.

Reliable

The program is free from design and coding errors.

Robust

The program does not crash easily with unexpected input.

Maintainable

A program is maintainable if future modifications can be performed easily and quickly.

Portable

The program is easily adapted to run in a different operating-system environment.

Efficient

The size and speed of execution should be in proportion to the scale of the problem that the program solves.

LET'S THINK ABOUT THIS

The features of the language and the skills of the programmers are both important in choosing a programming language to implement a software solution to a problem.

Some programs are still written in a low-level language, which is very time-consuming and error-prone. Why is a high-level language not always the best choice of language?

SOFTWARE DEVELOPMENT PROCESS – TESTING

INTRODUCTION

Testing can never show that a complex program is error-free, since the possible inputs that a program could be given are endless. The aim is to test the software as thoroughly as is possible given the constraints of time and money. Testing can show the presence of errors, but it can never prove that they are absent.

TYPES OF ERROR

Syntax Error

These are mistakes in the grammar of the programming language, reported by the translator since they are breaking the rules of the language and can't be translated. Examples:

1   Misspellings of language keywords: Prnt, Nexy I and so on.
2   Missing inverted commas: Picture1.Print "Hello
3   A For … Next loop with a For but no Next.

Run-time Error

These are errors that are not detected by the translator but are discovered when the program is run. A common run-time error occurs when the program is instructed to divide by zero, which will generate an error and crash the program. Another example is when a program attempts to read data from a file on disc, and the disc is not present in the disc drive. Good software should have error-trapping techniques to avoid these errors.

Logical Error

A program can translate error-free and have no run-time errors but still not give correct results if there is error in the logic of the instructions. For example, code could be written to add two numbers instead of multiplying them, or subtract two numbers the wrong way round.

DON'T FORGET

It is a common mistake to mix up a structured listing with a structured walkthrough. A structured walkthrough is a technique to locate errors in the code, but a structured listing is simply a formatted printout of the program code.

DON'T FORGET

Module Testing is also known as Integration Testing.
Acceptance Testing is also known as Beta Testing.

TECHNIQUES TO LOCATE AND REMOVE ERRORS

A structured walkthrough: involves following through the logic of the instructions line by line using a structured listing of the code. A structured listing is a formatted printout of the program code (indented loops, gaps between procedures and so on).

A dry run: involves stepping through the program instructions and manually working out on paper how the program variables are updated. A dry run can be used to locate logical errors in the program.

SYSTEMATIC TESTING

This involves a progression through testing subroutines to testing the whole system.

Component Testing: the first stage is to check that individual procedures and functions work by themselves.

Module Testing: once individual procedures and functions have been tested, the next stage is to test whether groups of procedures and functions successfully communicate with each other in modules.

contd

SYSTEMATIC TESTING contd

Subsystem Testing: the systematic testing then proceeds to test whether groups of modules work together as a unit in a subsystem.

System Testing: the whole system is tested to see if the subsystems communicate together as a unit.

Acceptance Testing: once the whole system has been tested by the developers, it is then tested by the clients in the situation in which it will be used.

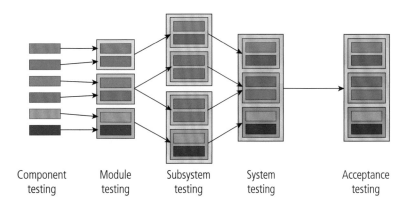

Component testing · Module testing · Subsystem testing · System testing · Acceptance testing

COMPREHENSIVE TESTING

Test data is chosen to test that the software can cope with as many cases as possible. Normal, boundary and exceptional data should be used to test the software.

Normal Data: One set of test data should be chosen to test that the software gives correct results for commonplace data without any unusual or extreme data.

Boundary Data: One set of test data should be chosen to see if the software can handle data on the limits.

Exceptional Data: One set of test data should be chosen for extreme cases in order to test the robustness of the software.

Example: A program enters seven exam marks as a percentage. The program then displays the number of marks in each grade (Fail 0–49, C 50–59, B 60–69, A 70–100).

The following sets of data would cover a good range of cases:
Normal test data   Marks 67, 34, 78, 56, 63, 40, 51
Boundary data   Marks 50, 100, 0, 60, 70, 49, 69
Exceptional data   Marks 144, –13, 50.5, 66A, 7 000 000, A, Polly

SOFTWARE DEVELOPMENT TOOL

A software development tool is an aid used to speed up the software development process.

Text editors provide a window in which source code can be entered and edited. They also provide automatic formatting such as indenting loops and using different colours for internal commentary.

A **translator** is a program that translates the source code into machine code and reports errors. High-level languages are translated by compilers and interpreters.

A **trace** is used by a programmer to manually step through the program line by line while watching how variables are updated in a trace table after each instruction has been executed.

A **breakpoint** is set as a marker alongside an instruction in the program. When the program reaches the breakpoint, program execution is suspended. The contents of the variables in the program can then be examined, typically by hovering over a variable in the code with the mouse pointer. A small text box displays the value of the variable.

LET'S THINK ABOUT THIS

In the coursework task, you will be required to write a program and use test data to show that the program is correct and robust. Explore the software development tools provided by the programming language that you use.

SOFTWARE DEVELOPMENT PROCESS – DOCUMENTATION AND EVALUATION

INTRODUCTION

Once the system has been implemented and fully tested, documentation is produced to help the users to learn how to use the system (user guide) as well as to help technical staff to install and maintain it (technical guide).

The documentation was traditionally in the form of paper manuals but is now also commonly provided in electronic form, where it can be more easily updated to incorporate updates to the software. Other advantages of providing online help are that it can be searched quickly with keywords and it is always available at the computer without the hassle of retrieving a manual.

Most software packages now provide a small manual to get the user started, usually with a tutorial section and an extensive online help facility.

DON'T FORGET

It is important to know the distinction between a user guide and a **technical guide**. The user guide describes how to use the features of the software, but the technical guide describes how to install and maintain it.

USER GUIDE

This documentation in the **user guide** is provided to teach the user how to use the features of the software. It will contain a description of these features and will often include tutorials to lead the user through typical tasks such as inserting a new record or reordering items of stock.

TECHNICAL GUIDE

This documentation is provided to help technical staff to maintain the software. A large company will have an IT department, which will take responsibility for the IT needs of the company. The following information would be included in this guide:

1 Details on how to install the software.

2 Information on the amount of RAM, hard disc capacity and processor requirements to run the software.

3 The version number of the software.

4 The guide should also contain a reference section on troubleshooting that will help the user to identify and correct any system errors.

 A lot of companies are now providing online support on the internet for their products. Use a search engine to find out the online support that is available for Microsoft Word.

OTHER DOCUMENTATION

The user guide and the technical guide are for the benefit of the clients to make full use of their system. There are many documents produced during the stages of the software development process. These documents are valuable as aids to the software development team, who may well be involved in future maintenance of the system. Good documentation is essential for future maintenance of the system, since, before changes can be made, the existing system must be fully examined and understood.

These items of documentation will include items such as structured listings, pseudocode, structure charts, results of test runs, drawings of screen layouts and so on.

DON'T FORGET

It is a common mistake to think that the user guide and the technical guide are the only items of documentation. Other items such as structured listings and pseudocode are equally important.

EVALUATION

When the software solution from analysis through to documentation is completed, it is important to evaluate it in terms of whether or not the original requirements have been met. Very often, the client is not happy with the final product; and this stage is important to rectify as many weaknesses as possible in the software before it is delivered in its final form.

The software is evaluated by judging it against a set of criteria.

A list of criteria is drawn up that can be used to evaluate the system as it proceeds through the stages of analysis, design, implementation, testing and documentation. Some examples are as follows:

- At the design stage, criteria can be constructed to measure the quality of the user interface.
  Does the client find the system user friendly?
  Can the software be learned to a competent level in three days?
  Is there consistency in the screen layouts?

- At the implementation stage, criteria can be constructed to evaluate the quality of the structured listing.
  Does the code use meaningful variable names?
  Is the code efficient?
  Does the code have sufficient internal commentary?

- At the testing stage, criteria can be constructed to evaluate whether the testing has been carried out comprehensively.
  Has testing been carried out with normal test data?
  Has test data been used to test whether the software is robust?

LET'S THINK ABOUT THIS

Documentation for a software solution exists in the form of a user guide, technical guide and documents produced during the development of the software.

Try to get hold of a software manual for a program that you use, and see what user and technical support it provides.

SOFTWARE DEVELOPMENT PROCESS – MAINTENANCE

INTRODUCTION

Even after a software system is complete and up and running, it will still have to undergo changes in the future to reflect the changing needs of the clients or even to remove previously undetected errors that come to light once the system is put to work.

TYPES OF MAINTENANCE ACTIVITY

Maintenance falls into **three** categories:

Corrective Maintenance

This involves removing errors in the software that were not detected during development but have come to light later when the clients are using the system. These errors should be removed by the development team.

DON'T FORGET

Students often confuse perfective and adaptive maintenance. Remember that perfective maintenance is adding new features to the program, whereas adaptive maintenance is modifying the program to cope with changes in the environment in which it runs.

Adaptive Maintenance

Over time, the software and hardware environment in which the system runs can change. For example, the operating system could be updated to a newer version, or different hardware devices such as barcode scanners or graph plotters could be employed.

The software system will require **adaptive maintenance** to adapt to these changes.

Perfective Maintenance

At some point in the future, the client may request enhancements to the software. This may be to modify the system by improving existing functions of the software or to add extra features to respond to changing needs of the system.

Costs

The client will not incur costs for corrective maintenance, since the developers have not met the legally binding contract stated in the software specification. However, any adaptive or perfective maintenance involves changes to the system outside the original agreement, and of course the client must pay for both of these maintenance activities.

FACTORS AFFECTING MAINTENANCE

Software development companies spend most of their time in maintaining existing software rather than developing new systems. Therefore it is very important to produce software that is relatively easy to maintain. The following factors will affect how easy it is to maintain a system.

Staff Mobility

People change jobs for a variety of reasons. The staff who are required to perform maintenance on the software are often not the staff who developed the original system. This makes maintenance more difficult, since the new staff will require time to familiarise themselves with a system that they did not create.

Poor Documentation

To modify a piece of software requires an understanding of how it works. Incomplete or out-of-date documentation acts as a hindrance to maintenance. Any modifications to a system should also be incorporated into the documentation for the system.

contd

FACTORS AFFECTING MAINTENANCE contd

Module Independence

Module independence is achieved by minimising the number of input and output parameters that the modules require and using local variables instead of global variables wherever possible.

Modules should be made as independent of each other as possible so that changes to one module do not require changes to all the other modules that share the same data. If modules are tightly coupled, then changes to one module would require tracking through the other modules which share the same data, thus increasing the time required for maintenance activity.

Programming Language

Some programming languages, by their nature, are easier to maintain than others. For example, a low-level-language program is much harder to modify than a high-level-language program.

Programming Style

Programs are often modified by a programmer who did not write the original code. Programs that are readable by using internal commentary, meaningful variable names, indented loops and so on are easier to understand and hence maintain than others which are not.

Hardware and Software Stability

If the hardware used by the software is being changed, or the operating system that the software runs on is being frequently upgraded to a new version, then the software may require modifications.

DON'T FORGET

The concept of module independence and how it is achieved is often badly explained by students in the exam. It is also important that you use independent modules in your program for the coursework task – so make sure you understand how to use local variables and parameters in your program code.

LET'S THINK ABOUT THIS

There are **three** types of maintenance activity: Corrective, Adaptive and Perfective.

During the lifetime of a system, approximately 20 per cent of time is spent on corrective maintenance, 20 per cent of time on adaptive maintenance and 60 per cent of time on perfective maintenance.

Future maintenance of a program is affected by factors including poor documentation, module independence, programming style and language, and staff mobility.

LANGUAGES AND ENVIRONMENTS 1

CLASSIFICATION OF PROGRAMMING LANGUAGES

Hundreds of programming languages have been developed to cater for the wide diversity of application areas in which they are applied. The requirements of a programming language being used to develop an artificial-intelligence program are very different from the requirements for a program being developed in numerical analysis. High-level languages can be classified into **four** groups according to their structure and purpose: **Procedural**, **Declarative**, **Event-driven** and **Scripting**.

CONTROL CONSTRUCTS

DON'T FORGET

There is more than one term used to describe the selection and repetition control constructs. Selection is sometimes referred to as branching, since the program branches to one or more instructions if a condition is true. Repetition is sometimes referred to as iteration or looping.

There are **three** basic **control constructs** used to define the order in which the instructions in a program are executed. These control constructs are found in all classifications of programming languages to control the flow of execution of the program code.

Sequencing

In sequencing, one instruction is executed after another. For example:

```
Let Length = 5
Let Breadth = 4
Let Height = 2
Let Volume = Length * Breadth * Height
Picture1.Print Volume
```

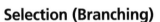

Selection (Branching)

In selection, one instruction or a set of instructions is executed if a condition is true. Two examples:

```
If Mark >= 50 THEN
        Picture1.Print "Pass"
        Let Passes = Passes + 1
Else
        Picture1.Print "Fail"
        Let Fails = Fails + 1
End If
```

```
Select Case Mark
Case Mark >= 70 AND Mark <= 100
        Picture1.Print "A Pass"
        Let APasses = APasses + 1
Case Mark >= 60 AND Mark < 70
        Picture1.Print "B Pass"
        Let BPasses = BPasses + 1
Case Mark >= 50 AND Mark < 60
        Picture1.Print "C Pass"
        Let CPasses = CPasses + 1
End Select
```

Repetition (Iteration)

In repetition, one instruction or a set of instructions is executed repeatedly.

There are **two** types of repetition:

Unconditional loop (fixed loop)
This type of loop repeats instructions a set number of times. For example:
```
For I = 1 To 12
    Picture1.Print "Hello"
Next I
```

Conditional loop
This type of loop repeats instructions until a condition is satisfied. For example:
```
Do
    Mark = Inputbox("Please enter your mark.")
    If Mark < 0 Or Mark > 100 Picture1.Print "Error!"
Loop Until Mark >= 0 AND Mark <= 100
```

PROCEDURAL LANGUAGES

Procedural languages have a clearly set start and end point to the program. The program follows a pre-defined pathway through the instructions to solve the problem.

contd

PROCEDURAL LANGUAGES contd

Typical features of a procedural language include:

Data types such as integer, real, string and Boolean.

Data structures such as arrays.

Arithmetic and logical operations such as +, –, * , /, AND, OR, NOT and so on.

Built-in functions such as Sin(), Sqr(), Left() and so on.

Subroutines (procedures and functions) with parameters to pass data in and out of the subroutines.

Sequencing, selection and repetition control constructs.

Pascal and C are examples of procedural languages.

DECLARATIVE LANGUAGES

A declarative language allows the programmer to create a **knowledge base** which contains facts and rules about a problem. A **query** is then used to interrogate the knowledge base and draw conclusions. These types of language are very good at logic but are not good at programs requiring calculations, since they have limited support for numeric data types.

Recursion

A form of looping known as recursion is found in declarative languages.

Recursion is the process of a procedure calling itself.

The procedure shown below adds 7 per cent to an account balance every time it is called up.

```
To AddInterest
Let Balance = Balance * 1.07
AddInterest
End Sub
```

The procedure shown above would repeat itself to infinity, so a mechanism has to be put in place to stop the procedure from calling itself.

```
Let Counter = 0
To AddInterest
Let Counter = Counter + 1
Let Balance = Balance * 1.07
AddInterest
If Counter = 10 then STOP
End Sub
```

The variable counter is set to 0 before the procedure is called and then incremented by 1 each time the procedure calls itself. The recursion loop ends when the counter reaches 10.

Declarative languages are used to develop expert systems in areas such as medical diagnosis and aircraft repair. Below is an example of the rules and facts used by an expert system.

Facts:

parent(william, rosie)	means that William is a parent of Rosie.
parent(connie, alan)	means that Connie is a parent of Alan.
female(rosie)	means that Rosie is a female
male(william)	means that William is a male.

Rules:

father(X, Y) :-parent(X, Y), male(X)	means that X is a father of Y if X is a parent of Y and X is a male.

A query such as father(X, rosie) would provide the result X=william.

Prolog is an example of a declarative language.

Explore declarative programming languages further by entering 'declarative language' into a search engine.

LET'S THINK ABOUT THIS

Programming languages can be classified into four groups according to their structure and characteristics. The flow of execution of the instructions in a program is achieved through sequence, selection and repetition control constructs.

LANGUAGES AND ENVIRONMENTS 2

EVENT-DRIVEN LANGUAGES

Event-driven programs do not have a specific pathway in which the program instructions are executed. Different parts of the program are evoked by events that take place during the running of the program. An event could be the user clicking on a command button, text being changed in a text box, a window being opened and so on.

The code in event-driven programs and procedural programs is similar, but the way in which it is executed is very different.

Visual Basic is an example of an event-driven language.

 Explore event-driven programming languages further by entering the keywords 'Wikipedia' and 'event-driven' into a search engine.

SCRIPTING LANGUAGES

Scripting languages are programming languages that are provided with an application package to allow the user to go beyond the features available in the application.

1 They allow an expert user to customise a package.

2 They can be used to automate repetitive tasks.

Macros

A **macro** is a set of actions performed by the user that have been recorded and can then be played back when required. The macro can be evoked by clicking on a button, or more quickly by allocating it a keyboard shortcut.

Many programs (like Microsoft Word and Microsoft Excel) allow the creation of macros. For example, a macro could be recorded to insert the user's name in italics in a header, automate a mail-merge, produce personalised letters and so on.

Once the macro has been recorded, it can be played back quickly and accurately.

The set of actions that are performed by the macro is stored as scripting language instructions which can then be viewed and edited.

For example, the following macro puts a name (left-aligned and italics) in a header and a page number (centred and bold) in a footer in a Word document.

```
Sub Macro1()
        ActiveWindow.ActivePane.View.SeekView = wdSeekCurrentPageHeader
        Selection.ParagraphFormat.Alignment = wdAlignParagraphLeft
        Selection.Font.Italic = wdToggle
        Selection.TypeText Text:="Wendy Wyper"
        ActiveWindow.ActivePane.View.SeekView = wdSeekCurrentPageFooter
        Selection.ParagraphFormat.Alignment = wdAlignParagraphCenter
        Selection.Font.Bold = wdToggle
        Selection.Fields.Add Range:=Selection.Range, Type:=wdFieldPage
        ActiveWindow.ActivePane.View.SeekView = wdSeekMainDocument
End Sub
```

VBA (Visual Basic for Applications) and JavaScript are examples of scripting languages.

COMPILERS AND INTERPRETERS

High-level languages require a compiler or an interpreter to translate the source code into machine code. One high-level-language instruction will translate into many machine-code instructions.

Compilers

A compiler translates the entire source code into machine code before the program is run.

1 The compiled program runs fast, since there is no translation at run time. (It has been translated before it is run.)

2 It produces a stand-alone machine-code program which can be executed by itself without the need of the source code and the compiler.

3 The source program will only be used again if the program needs to be modified.

4 Errors in the source code are reported when the program is compiled. Once the errors have been corrected, the complete program has to be compiled again before it can be run and tested.

Interpreters

An interpreter translates the source code one instruction at a time and executes it when the program is being run.

1 An interpreted program will run slower than a compiled program, since time is taken to translate the instructions while the program is being run.

2 An interpreter does not produce an independent machine-code program but always requires the interpreter and the source code to be loaded into main memory to run the program.

3 The interpreter is a less complicated and hence cheaper program than a compiler.

4 An interpreted program is easier to edit than a compiled program, since the program will stop at the first error, which can then be corrected immediately and allow the program to be run again.

DON'T FORGET

Interpreted languages are usually used to teach programming, since errors can be corrected quickly. Compiled languages are used to produce commercial programs, since they produce a faster-execution stand-alone program.

MODULE LIBRARIES

A **module library** is a collection of pre-written subroutines that are available to a programmer to speed up the software development process. Pre-written modules exist for algorithms that come up time and time again in programs such as sorting an array or validating an item of data. A lot of time can be gained by inserting a pre-written module into the program to perform these tasks.

Advantages of Module Libraries

1 Time is saved in not having to write the same programming code over and over again.

2 The module will have been tried and tested and therefore should be free from errors.

3 Complex and difficult programming algorithms can be evoked simply by calling an existing module written by an expert programmer.

The documentation for a module in a module library will include items such as:

1 a description of the function of the module

2 the parameters that are passed in and out of the module and their data types

3 the programming language that it is written in.

LET'S THINK ABOUT THIS

Find out how to record and play back some macros in the word-processing program that you use. You may find that you can save yourself time by automating some tasks.

The procedures and functions that you create in your programming work can be saved in your own personal module library, which will save you time when you come to the coursework task.

HIGH-LEVEL PROGRAMMING LANGUAGE CONSTRUCTS 1

VARIABLES

Data used by a program is stored in main-memory storage locations. A variable is the name that the program uses to identify the location that is storing an item of data. Using meaningful names for variables, such as Score1 and Length, makes the program more readable.

Declaring Variables

Most programming languages require variables to be declared before they are used. Declaring variables has advantages:

1 The translator can set aside areas of main memory to hold the data.

2 The program is more readable, since variables do not suddenly appear in instructions without an advance warning to the programmer.

DATA TYPES

Programming languages allow the creation of a variety of different **data types**. These data types exist to allow the programmer to control how items of data are stored in memory and to restrict the operations that can be performed on the data. Below are examples of common data types used in programming languages.

An **integer** variable stores a positive or negative whole number: for example, 0, 17, −3, 876
An integer is represented as a two's complement binary number.

A **real** variable stores fractional numbers: for example, 2.0, 3.9, −89.5432
A real number is represented as a floating-point binary number.

A **Boolean** variable stores only two values: True or False.

A **character** variable **(Char)** stores a single character, usually from the ASCII character set: for example, 'a', '@', '%', 'Y', '*'

A **string** variable stores a sequence of characters: for example, 'Monica Clinton', 'FAQ', 'Graceland' and so on.

ARRAYS

DON'T FORGET

An array is an example of a **data structure**. A data structure is a way of storing data in a computer so that it can be used efficiently.

An **array** is used to manipulate a group of data more easily than using independent variable names for each item of data. In an array, the group of data is given a name, and each element of the array is identified using a subscript. Arrays allow programs to be more readable and efficient. An array would be used to store data structures such as a list of 20 names or 120 exam marks.

The diagram below represents an array called Marks which stores five integer values.

	(0)	(1)	(2)	(3)	(4)
Marks	56	80	37	90	26

Marks (0) = 56, Marks (1) = 80 and so on.

STRING OPERATIONS

Concatenation

This is joining string variables together to make longer strings.
The operator for concatenation is usually the ampersand symbol (&).

contd

STRING OPERATIONS contd

For example, Print "Dog" & "ma" would give the string "Dogma".

Substrings

The Left, Right and Mid functions are used to return part of a string.

1 Left function
Returns a string containing a specified number of characters from the left-hand side of a
string: Left("Hello world", 4) returns "Hell", and Left("Hello world", 7) returns "Hello w".

2 Right function
Returns a string containing a specified number of characters from the right-hand side of a string:
Right("Partick Thistle", 2) returns "le", and Right("Partick Thistle", 11) returns "ick Thistle".

3 Mid function
Returns a string starting from a specified position in the string containing a specified number
of characters. If Mystring = "I made him an offer that he could not refuse", then
Mid(MyString, 3, 8) returns "made him" (starting at position 3 returns 8 characters)

FORMATTING OUTPUT

The format of the output of a program can be controlled using the Tab() function. For example,
the program below displays the squares and cubes of whole numbers from 1 to 6 in tabular form
using the Tab() function.

```
Private Sub Command1_Click()
Picture1.Print "Number"; Tab(10); "Square"; Tab(20); "Cube"
For i = 1 To 6
        Picture1.Print i; Tab(10); i * i; Tab(20); i * i * i
Next i
End Sub
```

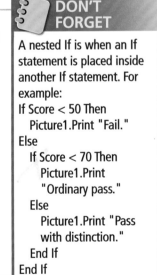

The Tab() function is used to display the headings then the results.
Note: Tab(10) sets the position for printing 10 characters from the left border of the PictureBox.

SELECT CASE

Select Case is used when the program is required to branch in several directions depending upon
the value of an expression. For example:

```
Select Case Mark
Case 0 To 49
    Print "Fail"
Case 50 To 59
    Print "Grade C"
Case 60 To 69
    Print "Grade B"
Case 70 To 100
    Print "Grade A"
End select
```

The same logic could be achieved with nested If statements but would make the code much less
readable.

LET'S THINK ABOUT THIS

A programmer controls how the variables in a program are stored by using different data types.
String variables can be broken down into substrings using the Left, Right and Mid functions. The
Select Case statement is preferable to several If statements to control multiple branches in a program.

HIGH-LEVEL PROGRAMMING LANGUAGE CONSTRUCTS 2

SCOPE OF VARIABLES

The aim in good programming is to limit the scope of program variables as far as possible. This means that the effect of any changes to the variable during modifications to the program need be traced through only a part of the program, making maintenance much easier.

A **local** variable only exists within the subroutine (procedure or function) in which it is declared. It can only be changed within that subroutine and will not be recognised by any other subroutine.

A **global** variable is recognised by all the subroutines within the program. It can be changed by any subroutine in the program. The aim is to minimise the number of global variables, since any change to a global variable in one subroutine must be traced through every other subroutine to see how they are affected.

PROCEDURES AND FUNCTIONS

Programs are modularised by breaking them down into subroutines.

This avoids unnecessary duplication of code and makes the design easier to manage and understand.

Procedures

A procedure produces an effect, for example sorting a list of marks, displaying a menu on the screen and so on. Shown below is the definition of a procedure which calculates the perimeter and area of a rectangle and displays the results.

```
Sub RectangleFacts(Length, Breadth)
'This procedure finds the perimeter and area of a rectangle and displays the results.
Dim Perimeter As Single
Dim Area As Single

Let Perimeter = 2 * (Length + Breadth)
Let Area = Length * Breadth
Picture1.Print "The perimeter of the rectangle is " & Perimeter
Picture1.Print "The area of the rectangle is " & Area
End Sub
```

The procedure is then used in the program with statements such as:
Call RectangleFacts(L, B), Call RectangleFacts(3, 8) and so on.

Functions

A **function** returns a single value, for example returning the mode of an array of numbers, returning the number of vowels in a string and so on. Shown below is the definition of a function to return the maximum value in an integer array.

```
Function Max(Scores() As Integer) As Integer
'This function returns the highest value in an array of integers.
Dim Max As Integer
Let Max = Scores(0)
For i = 1 To 9
        If Scores(i) > Max Then
                Let Max = Scores(i)
        End If
Next i
End Function
```

contd

PROCEDURES AND FUNCTIONS contd

The function is then used in the program with statements such as:
Let Highest=Max(Numbers()), Picture1.Print "The best mark was ";Max(Marks()) and so on.

PARAMETERS

A **parameter** is a variable or value that is passed into or out of a subroutine.

Actual and Formal Parameters

The parameters which are passed into the subroutine when it is called from another part of the program are called the **actual** parameters.

The parameters which are used in the subroutine definition are called the **formal** parameters.

Passing Parameters by Reference and by Value

There are two methods of passing parameters: by reference and by value.

Passing parameters by reference is used when the value being passed in is to be updated and passed back out again. (The variable itself is passed to the subroutine so that any changes to the variable will change the variable.)

Passing parameters by value is used when a value is passed into a subroutine but does not require to be passed out. (The subroutine makes a copy of the variable so that any changes to the copy of the variable will not change the variable.)

Example

The program shown below asks for the length and breadth of a rectangle and then calculates the area and displays the result.

```
Dim L As Integer
Dim B As Integer

Sub GetSides(ByRef Length As Integer, ByRef Breadth As Integer)
'Get the length and breadth of the rectangle
Let Length = InputBox("Please enter the length of the rectangle.")
Let Breadth = InputBox("Please enter the breadth of the rectangle.")
End Sub
```

Procedure Declaration
Length + Breadth are
Formal Parameters

```
Function Area(ByVal Length As Integer, ByVal Breadth As Integer) As Integer
'Calculate the area of the rectangle
Let Area = Length * Breadth
End Function
```

Function Declaration
Length + Breadth are
Formal Parameters

```
Private Sub Command1_Click()
Call GetSides(L, B)
End Sub
```

Procedure Call
L + B are Actual Parameters

```
Private Sub Command2_Click()
Picture1.Print "The area of the rectangle is "; Area(L, B)
End Sub
```

Function Call
L + B are Actual Parameters

Note: In the GetSides procedure, the parameters Length and Breadth are both passed by reference, since the changes made to the parameters have to be passed out.

In the Area function, the parameters Length and Breadth are both passed by value, since the changes made to the parameters do not have to be passed out.

DON'T FORGET

Arrays are always passed by reference to subroutines, since making a copy of a large data structure such as an array would use up too much memory.

LET'S THINK ABOUT THIS

The coursework task always requires a program that passes parameters in and out of subroutines. Learn how to do this in your programming language. Always use a function and not a procedure to return a single value such as an average or a maximum.

STANDARD ALGORITHMS

DON'T FORGET

Although finding maximum and finding minimum are covered as two separate algorithms, they are almost identical.

INTRODUCTION

Many **algorithms**, such as sorting a list or finding a maximum, appear repeatedly in programs. These are called standard algorithms. This course covers four standard algorithms used by programmers: Linear Search, Counting Occurrences, Finding Maximum and Finding Minimum.

LINEAR SEARCH

The algorithm begins searching for a value at the first item in a list and continues searching through each item of the list in turn.

The algorithm shown below searches the entire list from start to finish and stops only when the end of the list is reached.

1. position=1
2. prompt the user for the search value
3. do
4.   if item(position) = search value then
5.   output search value and position
6.   end if
7.   position = position + 1
8. loop until position > no. of items in list

The following improved algorithm makes use of a **condition** that will stop the search if the search value is found and will not continue to the end of the list.

1.   set found to false
2.   position = 1
3.   prompt the user for the search value
4.   do
5.   if item(position) = search value then
6.   set found to true
7.   output search value and position
8.   else
9.   position = position + 1
10.   end if
11.   loop until (found = true) or (position > no. of items in list)
12.   if found = false then
13.   display message not found
14.   end if

COUNTING OCCURRENCES

This algorithm counts how often a value occurs in a list of items. It does the following:

1 sets a counter to zero
2 searches a list for the occurrence of a search value
3 increments the counter by 1 each time the search value is found.

Counting occurrences of a search value in a list of items:

1. counter = 0
2. prompt the user for the search value
3. for position = 1 to no. of items in list
4.   if search value equals item(position) then
5.   counter = counter +1
6.   end if

contd

COUNTING OCCURRENCES contd

7. end of loop
8. display counter

FINDING MAXIMUM VALUE

This algorithm is used to find the maximum value in a list. It does the following:

1 a max variable is set to the first item in the list
2 each item in the list is compared to the max to see if it is bigger
3 every time the item in the list is bigger, then the max is updated to that item.

Finding the maximum in a list of items:

1. set maximum to first item in the list
2. for position = 2 to no. of items in list
3.   if item(position) > maximum then
4.   set maximum to item(position)
5.   end if
6. end of loop
7. display maximum value

FINDING MINIMUM VALUE

This algorithm is virtually identical to finding the maximum value, only every time the item in the list is smaller, then the minimum is updated to that item.

Finding the minimum in a list of items:

1. set minimum to first item in the list
2. for position = 2 to no. of items in list
3.   if item(position) < minimum then
4.   set minimum to item(position)
5.   end if
6. end of loop
7. display minimum value

DON'T FORGET

Finding the maximum/ minimum value in a list of items is not the same as finding the position of the maximum/minimum. Study these algorithms carefully to understand the difference fully.

FINDING THE POSITION OF THE MAXIMUM/MINIMUM

Sometimes, there is the requirement to find the position of the maximum or minimum item in the list.

Finding the position of the maximum in a list of items:

1. set maxposition to 1
2. for position = 2 to no. of items in list
3.   if item(position) > item(maxposition) then
4.   set maxposition to position
5.   end if
6. end of loop
7. display maxposition

LET'S THINK ABOUT THIS

There are four standard algorithms, any of which may be required for the programming part of the coursework task. Use the logic of these algorithms in the subroutines of your program.

A standard algorithm called a binary search is efficient at searching for a value in a long list. Research the binary search algorithm.

SOFTWARE DEVELOPMENT

EXAM-STYLE QUESTIONS

QUESTION 1

A school enlists a software development company to produce a computer system to run its library.

A systems analyst visits the school, calls a meeting with the headmaster and some senior staff and explains that the first step is to examine the existing system.

(a) Describe **two** techniques that can be used at the analysis stage to examine the existing system.

(b) The next stage of the development stage is the design stage. **Name** and **describe** the document that the design team will use as a basis for the design of the software.

(c) (i) The program is to be written by a team of six programmers.
Why is a structure diagram useful in allocating tasks to the programmers?
(ii) Name another item of documentation produced at the design stage.

(d) The programming team made use of module libraries to develop the software.
Give **two** reasons why the use of module libraries should speed up program development.

(e) The final solution was tested to ensure that it was **correct** and **robust**.
Explain the terms 'correct' and 'robust'.

(2, 2, 2, 2, 2)

QUESTION 2

Testing of software can never show that the software is error-free but should be as comprehensive as possible given time and money constraints. Often, independent test groups are brought in to test the programs.

(a) Why do software development companies employ independent test groups to test software rather than let the software be tested by the programmers who wrote it?

(b) A program subroutine enters **six** test scores in the range 0–25 and calculates the number of fails (0–12), passes (13–22) and passes with distinction (23–25).
The subroutine should validate the scores in the range 0–25.
Give **three** sets of test data that could be used to test this subroutine fully, giving a reason why you chose each set of test data.

(c) For each set of test data, give the expected output from the subroutine.

(1, 6, 3)

QUESTION 3

An integrated package has word-processing, spreadsheet, database and graphics sections. The package has a built-in scripting language and macro facility.

(a) Explain what is meant by a scripting language.

(b) One user of the integrated package always puts his name as a header and the date as a footer on all his documents. Describe an efficient method of adding the header and footer to the documents.

(c) Programs in the field of artificial intelligence are created using declarative languages. Describe **two** features of a declarative language.

(d) Some languages have both an interpreted and a compiled version. Explain the advantage that having both versions will have on:
(i) the speed of development of software
(ii) the quality of the software produced.

(2, 2, 2, 4)

QUESTION 4

A program has been written to process scores by the competitors in an ice-skating competition. Each skater receives a score in the range 0.0–6.0 from each of six judges. A skater's overall score is calculated from the total of the six scores minus the best and the worst scores.

Judge	1	2	3	4	5	6
Score	5.2	5.5	4.9	5.2	5.7	5.3

Overall score = 5.2 + 5.5 + 4.9 + 5.2 + 5.7 + 5.3 − 5.7 − 4.9 = **21.2**

(a) The program validates each score entered by the judges using a complex condition to control a conditional loop. Describe the complex condition.

(b) A subroutine called **final_score** calculates the overall score for a skater from the six judges' scores. State whether the final_score subroutine is a procedure or a function, and justify your answer.

(c) The final_score subroutine uses the input parameter list_of_scores.
   (i) Explain why an integer data type is not suitable for this parameter, and give a suitable data type.
   (ii) State whether the parameter list_of_scores should be passed by reference or by value, and explain your answer.

(d) This program could have used six separate variables or a one-dimensional array to store the judges' scores for an ice skater. What are the advantages of a one-dimensional array over six variables in terms of:
   (i) future maintenance;
   (ii) efficiency;
   (iii) data storage requirements?

(1, 2, 4, 3)

QUESTION 5

A program is used to enter and process the results of a cross-country running competition. The program enters the name, sex, year group, age and finishing time of the competitors. The program stores the details for 80 competitors using different **data types**.

(a) (i) Explain the term 'data type'.
   (ii) What data structure and data type would be used within the program to store the names of the 80 competitors?

(b) Four standard algorithms are:
   1 Linear Search
   2 Counting Occurrences
   3 Finding Maximum
   4 Finding Minimum.

   Which standard algorithms would the program use to find:
   (i) the number of girls in the race;
   (ii) the best time for the race?

(c) On the day of the race, the finishing times of the 80 competitors are entered into the program. An athlete who runs the race in less than 12 minutes gains a star award. Using a design notation with which you are familiar, write an algorithm which would find the number of athletes who gained a star award.

(d) Why would the cross-country running program not have been created using a declarative language?

(3, 2, 4, 1)

SOFTWARE DEVELOPMENT
ANSWERS

QUESTION 1

2 × 1 mark for each description	**(a)**	Any two from: Interview managers and staff. Make observation notes. Examine existing documentation.
1 mark for naming the document	**(b)**	Software specification. 1 mark for description. A legally binding document that specifies exactly what the software should do.
1 mark	**(c) (i)**	The structure diagram splits the program up into smaller parts that can then be allocated to individual programmers.
1 mark	**(ii)**	Pseudocode, designs of screen layouts.
2 × 1 mark for each reason	**(d)**	Time is not spent writing the modules. The modules are tried and tested, and time is not wasted removing errors.
2 × 1 mark for each description	**(e)**	'Correct' means that the program meets the specification. 'Robust' means that the program does not easily crash with unexpected input.

QUESTION 2

1 mark	**(a)**	The programmers would be biased in not showing the presence of errors. Also, the independent test group would be experienced in locating errors.
3 × 1 mark for each set of test data 3 × 1 mark for each reason	**(b)**	Test1 12, 23, 14, 20, 15, 7 Reason To test if the program can give correct results for normal data. Test2 12, 0, 23, 13, 25, 22 Reason To test if the program gives correct results for boundary data. Test3 27, −3, 144, A, Polly, K9 Reason To test if the program can cope with exceptions without crashing.
3 × 1 mark for each output	**(e)**	Test1 Output 2 fails, 3 passes, 1 pass with distinction. Test2 Output 2 fails, 2 passes, 2 passes with distinction. Test3 Output The program should return an error message and ask for the data to be re-entered.

QUESTION 3

2 × 1 mark for each point	**(a)**	A scripting language works alongside an application package. It is a programming language that allows the user to customise the package and automate repetitive tasks.
2 marks	**(b)**	The user can record the action of entering the header and footer in a macro and then play it back with a keyboard shortcut or mouse click as often as required.
2 × 1 mark for each feature	**(c)**	Any two from: A set of rules and facts is held in a knowledge base. A query is used to interrogate the knowledge base. Recursion is a procedure which calls itself.
2 marks	**(d) (i)**	The interpreted version allows the software to be developed more quickly, since errors can be corrected more easily than with the compiled version.

contd

QUESTION 3 contd

(ii) The compiled version allows a stand-alone machine-code program to be produced which will run faster than the interpreted program and does not require the source code or translator to run it.

2 marks

QUESTION 4

(a) Score>=0 AND Score<=6.

1 mark

(b) A function.
1 mark for reason.
This subroutine is a function, since it returns a single value.

1 mark

(c) (i) The integer data type cannot store decimal fractions such as 5.3.

1 mark

REAL would be a suitable data type, since it can store decimal fractions.

1 mark

(ii) The parameter should be passed by reference.

1 mark

An array is always passed by reference, since passing it by value would require a copy to be made of a large amount of data.

1 mark for reason

(d) (i) Maintenance would be easier, since the data is manipulated as a unit so that changes to the program can be effected much quicker than modifying ten independent variables.

1 mark

(ii) The program would be more efficient, since the data in the array can be manipulated in a loop rather than a separate instruction for each variable.

1 mark

(iii) There would be no change to the storage requirements, since ten items of data are being stored in each method.

1 mark

QUESTION 5

(a) (i) A data type defines how an item of data is represented in memory and restricts the operations that can be performed on the data.

1 mark

(ii) An array data structure.

1 mark for correct data structure.

The names would be stored in the STRING data type.

1 mark for correct data type.

(b) (i) Counting Occurrences.

1 mark

(ii) Finding Minimum.

1 mark

(c)
1. Set counter to 0
2. For position = 1 to 80
3.   If time(position) is less than 12 then
4.   counter = counter +1
5.   End if
6. Next position
7. Display counter

4 marks
1 mark should be taken off for each missing or incorrect instruction.

(d) A declarative language is good at programs requiring logic and decisions but not so good at storing numerical data and performing operations on numerical data.

1 mark

THE DEVELOPMENT OF ARTIFICIAL INTELLIGENCE 1

HUMAN INTELLIGENCE AND ARTIFICIAL INTELLIGENCE

Definition of Intelligence

Most people can recognise intelligence, but it is difficult to come up with a definition of intelligence that most people would agree on. Part of the problem is that there are many aspects associated with intelligent behaviour; however, it is generally agreed that the following are features of intelligent behaviour.

Language
The ability to communicate through language.

Learning
The ability to learn from experience and adapt accordingly.

Cognitive ability
The ability to have conscious intellectual activity such as thinking, reasoning and imagining to collate facts and draw conclusions.

Problem-solving skills
The ability to apply known knowledge to respond to an unfamiliar situation.

Memory
The ability to retain and recall information.

Creativity
The ability to be inventive, imaginative and resourceful.

Definition of Artificial Intelligence

Artificial intelligence (AI) is a computer system performing a task that would require intelligence if performed by a human being.

There is an argument that, since AI systems are simply programs written by human beings, they have no originality in their operation and therefore do not exhibit real intelligence.

Against this argument, it can be said that, even at present, AI programs are demonstrating aspects of intelligence to great success in areas such as playing chess, expert systems, natural language processing and so on – and this is only the beginning!

> **DON'T FORGET**
>
> There is much difference of opinion on what defines human intelligence, since different aspects of intelligence are seen as more important than others by different people. Therefore it is very difficult to clearly define artificial intelligence in the absence of a clear definition of human intelligence.

TURING TEST

When AI programs first appeared in the mid-twentieth century, there was much debate about whether a machine could ever be programmed to demonstrate really intelligent behaviour. The **Turing test** was proposed in 1950, by a Cambridge mathematician called Alan Turing, to determine if an AI program was truly intelligent.

In the Turing test, the tester is put in a room which has two computer terminals. One terminal is used to communicate with a human, and the other terminal is used to communicate with a computer program. Turing said that, if the tester can't tell which is the human and which is the computer program, then the computer program has passed the test for artificial intelligence.

Flaws in the Turing Test

1 Human intelligence can vary dramatically from person to person, so that it may be very difficult to choose the right people for the Turing testing process. The test depends on the intelligence of the interrogator as much as on the intelligence of the interrogated human.

`contd`

TURING TEST contd

2 The test operates in a restricted domain and is only testing a limited aspect of intelligence. It can be argued that the Turing test is aimed at natural language processing and is not testing other aspects of intelligence such as creativity and problem-solving.

 There is plenty of information on the Turing test on the internet and the debate that it stimulates. Research the Turing test further by entering the phrase 'Turing test' into a search engine.

KNOWLEDGE REPRESENTATION

Methods are used to describe what is known about a problem in terms of facts and rules. This can be done through diagrams such as semantic nets or a list of facts and rules which would be used in a declarative language.

Restricted Domain

In order to model a situation, it is necessary to clearly define the limits and boundaries of the problem. The knowledge known about a situation must be limited to make sure that search times are practical and to fit in with the amount of computer memory available to store rules and facts.

Semantic Nets

This is a diagram that shows the entities in a system and how they are linked. Semantic nets make it easier for a human to take in the knowledge known about a problem by presenting it pictorially, but in a large problem the number of entities and links can be too complex to take in. The example below shows a simple semantic net representing the classification of some birds and reptiles.

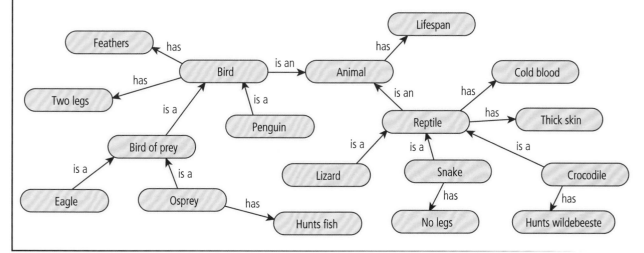

LET'S THINK ABOUT THIS

Write down seven features that you think are important aspects of human intelligence such as problem-solving, memory, imagination and so on. Ask several people to put them into order from the most important to the least important. Analyse the results thus:

1 Give the number-one choice a score of 7, the second choice a score of 6 and so on.

2 Calculate the total score for each aspect of intelligence.

3 Rank the seven features in order of importance from the highest total score to the lowest total score.

THE DEVELOPMENT OF ARTIFICIAL INTELLIGENCE 2

LISP AND PROLOG

Logic Programming

Declarative languages are used to implement logic programming. These types of programming languages have already been covered in the Software Development chapter in the Languages and Environments 1 spread.

Declarative languages can be classified as functional and logical.

LISP is a functional programming language which applies functions to data structures.

Prolog is a logic programming language which codes knowledge about a problem which is used to solve problems that are based upon logic.

 Explore the LISP and Prolog programming languages further by entering the keywords 'Wikipedia', 'LISP' and 'Prolog' into a search engine.

Differences between a Declarative and a Procedural Language

Declarative programming languages solve a problem by stating rules and facts about a problem where the order of execution is determined only when the program is executed.

A procedural language has a set algorithm where the order of execution of the instructions is pre-defined from start to finish.

A declarative language lists facts and rules about a problem but not how to solve the problem, whereas a procedural language has more control over how the problem is solved.

DON'T FORGET

Procedural languages are also known as imperative languages because they solve a problem by following a series of commands.

SUCCESS AND FAILURES OF GAME-PLAYING PROGRAMS

Artificial intelligence has been applied successfully to many well-known games. These include noughts and crosses, draughts, Connect 4, chess and so on. The success of AI in playing games is highlighted by chess, where even the early programs were able to beat 99 per cent of the world's chess players. These AI programs work by storing the game position, analysing the outcomes of all the permutations of possible plays and then choosing a move that maximises the chances of winning.

Some games, such as backgammon which uses two dice, make it much harder for the computer to be sure of success because of the random element introduced by throwing the dice.

The difficulties in developing AI programs to play games include:

1 representing the current state of the game

2 some games are very complex and require a lot of rules to be defined

3 the number of possible moves increases rapidly when looking several steps ahead

4 finding a way of evaluating moves to maximise the prospects of winning.

LANGUAGE PROCESSING

Eliza

Eliza was a program that responded to questions entered by the user in such a way as to give the impression of understanding their meaning. In reality, Eliza responded to keywords and had a limited variety of responses, and could easily be confused or misled. The original writer of Eliza intended it to be a parody of a psychiatrist, since it rephrased many of the user's statements as questions.

contd

LANGUAGE PROCESSING contd

An example of an 'Eliza' conversation is shown below.

Eliza: Hello. I am ELIZA. How can I help you?
You: I want to be a millionaire.
Eliza: Why do you want to be a millionaire?
You: So I can live in a big house.
Eliza: Can you elaborate on that?
You: A big house with 10 bedrooms and a swimming pool.
Eliza: Please go on.
You: I am tired of talking to you.
Eliza: How long have you been tired of talking to me?
You: Since you stopped paying attention.
Eliza: Oh, I stopped paying attention.
You: Yes, you did.
Eliza: Are you sure?
You: Goodbye.

The Eliza program is able to hold a conversation (doing better than some humans) but cannot be considered to be intelligent, since it merely looks up keywords and phrases in a lookup table and does not show any ability to make decisions or be imaginative.

SHRDLU

This program made use of natural language-processing techniques to allow the user to use English commands to manipulate coloured building blocks. SHRDLU had a memory that allowed it to remember names given to objects and their arrangement so that it could answer questions about them. This program worked successfully in a very limited world where the positioning of the objects in locations was able to be described by around 50 words.

Although SHRDLU appears to be able to communicate with the user, it works in a restricted area and is not able to think for itself or to justify its responses.

Chatterbots

More powerful programs called chatterbots have been developed which simulate a more intelligent conversation with a human being than Eliza did. These are increasingly being used by companies as a first point of contact on a website or over the telephone to provide support, intelligently direct inquiries and so on.

EFFECTS OF HARDWARE DEVELOPMENTS ON AI

The real world is very complex, and therefore to model it on a computer requires fast processors and high-capacity RAM and backing store devices to store and manipulate the data. Early AI systems were limited in the hardware performance necessary for an AI system, and consequently these systems were crude and slow.

The advent of faster processors has allowed searches for keywords to be performed more quickly, and more memory has allowed large amounts of data to be stored in main memory for faster direct access.

Parallel processing

In-depth searches in AI can require a virtually limitless number of paths to be evaluated in the search for a match. Parallel processing is a computer system with multiple processors, each of which can be processing data simultaneously and speed up the time required to find a solution.

LET'S THINK ABOUT THIS

Get hold of a copy of the language-processing program 'Eliza' and judge how intelligently it converses with you. Try to confuse it and expose its inflexibility and lack of true intelligence.

APPLICATIONS OF ARTIFICIAL INTELLIGENCE 1

ARTIFICIAL NEURAL SYSTEMS (ANS)

An **artificial neural system** is a network of artificial neurons that models the way that human neurons are connected and trigger signals to each other. An ANS is similar in operation to the neurons in the human brain, but the ANS has many times fewer neurons than the human brain and is therefore not nearly as complex. The structure of a neural net consists of:

1 **Artificial neurons**
2 **Links** connecting the artificial neurons
3 **Weight** given to each artificial neuron, so that it 'fires' if its input value exceeds a certain threshold
4 **Layers** which generate signals beginning with the inner layer, through a series of hidden layers to the output layer.

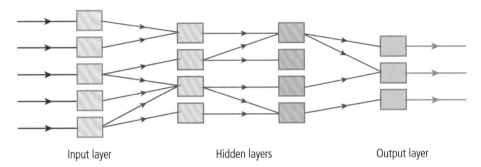

Input layer   Hidden layers   Output layer

Learning through the Iterative Method

Neural networks can be trained by running tests to check the initial weight settings of the artificial neurons. Test data is entered, and the output is compared with a known expected output. The weight settings can then be altered to give the required output, and the process is repeated until the output agrees with the expected output.

Software Model and Hard-wired

Neural networks can be implemented in software, or by hardware where the artificial neurons are hard-wired into a circuit board.

Applications of ANS

ANSs are successful in application areas such as financial forecasting, OCR (optical character recognition), weather forecasting and indeed any situations where the system is learning by repeatedly comparing its own output with the correct output.

VISION SYSTEMS

The ability of a computer to recognise an image is still limited, but intelligent vision systems have a huge potential in many areas such as bomb disposal, assembling components in manufacture, space exploration and so on.

The Main Stages of Computer Vision

Image recognition by a computer system proceeds through the following five stages:

1 **Image acquisition:** an input device such as a digital camera is used to capture the image.

2 **Signal processing:** the image is converted into digital data so that it can be stored and processed by the computer.

> **DON'T FORGET**
>
> The method used by a neural network to learn is another example in this course of iteration, where an earlier task is repeated in the light of experience gained at a later stage in order to improve a solution.

contd

VISION SYSTEMS contd

3 Edge detection: the digital data is analysed to look for areas where there is a sudden change in the colour of pixels which indicate edges. This analysis produces a simpler outline of the image as defined by its edges.

4 Object recognition: the objects in the image are identified by comparing them with known objects using pattern matching.

5 Image understanding: the identified objects in the image are related to each other so that sense can be made of the whole image.

Problems of Interpreting 2D Objects as 3D Objects

Identifying 3D objects from a 2D image has several difficulties.

1 Parts of the object may be hidden by other objects.
2 There may be shadow on objects which fools the system into seeing edges that do not exist.
3 The object may be being viewed from an unusual angle.
4 The object to be identified may not be in the known database.

NATURAL LANGUAGE PROCESSING (NLP)

NLP is the process of a computer system recognising and responding intelligently to written or spoken language. The complexity and ambiguity of human languages makes this a difficult and problematic task, but eventually it could mean that you will be able to address your computer as though you were addressing another person.

Natural language processing proceeds through four main stages:

1 Speech recognition: the sounds or text are input into the computer, and letters and words are identified.

2 Natural language understanding (NLU): the combination of words is given meaning.

3 Natural language generation: this is the process of generating natural language from information held in a database.

4 Speech synthesis: the production of spoken or textual output.

Difficulties in NLP

1 Ambiguity of meaning: often, a phrase can be interpreted in more than one way. For example, the phrase 'The duchess can't bear children' can mean that the duchess does not like children or that the duchess is infertile.

2 Similar-sounding words: words can sound the same but have a different meaning – for example, sight and site, Doug and dug.

3 Grammatical inconsistencies: the grammar in human language is complex and inconsistent. It is very difficult to get a computer system to recognise all the variations.

4 Changing language: the meaning of words can change over a period of time. For example, 'cool' has changed its meaning.

Applications of NLP

NLP has a huge potential in application areas such as language translation (French to English, and so on), automated telephone inquiries, NL search engines and so on.

LET'S THINK ABOUT THIS

Ambiguity is one of the main difficulties in natural language processing. It is very easy to write a sentence that is ambiguous. For example, 'I met a man with a dog who licked my face' can be interpreted in two ways. Make up some sentences that can have more than one meaning.

APPLICATIONS OF ARTIFICIAL INTELLIGENCE 2

SMART/EMBEDDED TECHNOLOGY

A smart/embedded system is a combination of hardware and intelligent software that is used to control devices such as car engines and domestic appliances. Embedded systems can operate autonomously and save time and money.

For example, smart technology in a car can monitor the system and inform the driver when an oil change is required, the correct speed to drive at to optimise fuel consumption, diagnose and report faults and so on.

INTELLIGENT ROBOTS

An **intelligent robot** is capable of processing input and making decisions that would normally require human intelligence. A dumb robot can be programmed to perform a task but would not be able to adapt to new situations and environments or have the ability to learn.

For example, a robot could be programmed to paint a car part on an assembly line but would blindly continue to spray paint even if the part was missing. An intelligent robot is fitted with sensors and has the ability to adapt to this situation and show 'intelligence'.

Social Implications

There is certain to be an increase in society in the number of robots and the variety of tasks that they perform. The use of robots is already spreading into areas such as playing the piano from the sheet music, hairdressing, medical operation assistance, bomb disposal and so on.

Legal Implications

There are legal implications in terms of attributing blame when accidents occur. For example, what happens when the owner of a carpet-vacuuming robot sucks up the cat? The owner of the robot, as well as the manufacturer and the programmer, all have a responsibility. Manufacturers can address these issues by:

1 insisting that the owner signs a disclaimer document
2 putting warnings on the robots such as flashing lights and sirens.

Practical Problems

Intelligent robots require a lot of processor power to make sense of their environment in a way that humans take for granted. Other problems:

1 Robots can't operate without a power supply.
2 Lack of mobility.
3 Vision recognition, as you have seen, is very complex and has its own difficulties.
4 Navigating around objects and planning a path.

These problems will be overcome as the technology evolves with faster processors, increased memory, better programming languages and programmers, smaller power supplies and so on.

DON'T FORGET

The Higher Computing course is not all about technology issues. You will be asked questions in the exam on social and legal issues as well.

EXPERT SYSTEMS

An expert system is a program that contains the combined knowledge of experts in a particular field, such as medicine or car mechanics, and can use this information to give a diagnosis or advice on that subject.

The Components of an Expert System

Knowledge base
This component contains the rules and facts about the problem.

contd

EXPERT SYSTEMS contd

Inference engine

This component determines what input to prompt for from the user and looks for matches with the user's query in the knowledge base (usually with a depth-first search) to draw a conclusion.

Explanatory interface with justification

This component takes the user input and gives an explanation (justification) of how it reached a decision or conclusion.

Expert System Shell

An expert system shell has all the structure of an expert system, but the knowledge base is empty. This cuts down on the development time for a system, since the user interface, inference engine, programming code and so on are already in place, and all that is required is the entering of the facts and rules into the knowledge base.

Applications of Expert Systems

Expert systems are used in medicine, law, machine repair, geological survey analysis and so on.

Advantages of Expert Systems

Cost-effectiveness

It will be cheaper to use an expert system than to pay for the advice of a human expert.

Consistency

The diagnosis or advice will be more consistent than a human.

Portability

An expert system can be carried around virtually anywhere and run on a laptop with its own power supply.

Disadvantages of Expert Systems

Narrow domain

There is a restricted area of information.

Lack of common sense

The expert system will not be able to respond to unexpected input or identify errors that would be obvious to a human.

Need for expertise to set up and maintain

The information for the knowledge base will have to be gathered from several experts and regularly updated.

Inflexibility and inability to acquire new knowledge

An expert system does not have the adaptability of a human or the ability to learn from experience.

Moral Issues

There is the issue of whether it is right that a machine should be contributing to life-and-death decisions.

Legal Issues

There is the matter of who is responsible when the advice given by an expert system is wrong. The main thing is that an expert system should only be used as a helpful tool and that it is the human who makes the actual decision. To address these issues, manufacturers often include a disclaimer stating that it is the user who is responsible for the decisions.

DON'T FORGET

An expert system differs from an artificial neural network in that an expert system is given all the facts and rules and can justify its advice, whereas an artificial neural network is given details from which it is trained and learns, and it can't justify or explain its advice.

Research legal issues about expert systems by entering the keywords 'expert system' and 'disclaimer' into a search engine.

LET'S THINK ABOUT THIS

Expert systems exist to help in financial planning and to advise on the buying and selling of shares on the stock market. Research the use of expert systems in business and finance.

SEARCH TECHNIQUES

BREADTH FIRST AND DEPTH FIRST

In AI, a brute-force search is a problem-solving technique where all possible solutions are examined in turn until a match is found. Breadth first and depth-first searches are two examples of brute-force search techniques.

Breadth first and depth first are two search techniques used to determine the order in which the nodes are visited in looking for a goal state to be found.

The search tree shown below can be used to compare a breadth-first and a depth-first search technique in the order in which they visit the nodes.

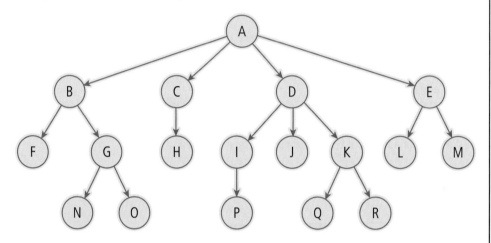

Breadth First

In this search technique, each horizontal layer (starting with the top layer and ending with the bottom layer) of the search tree is searched from left to night in turn.

The order of visiting the nodes in the search tree above is:

A, B, C, D, E, F, G, H, I, J, K, L, M, N, O, P, Q, R.

Memory

The breadth-first search technique is very costly on memory requirements because the entire tree must be stored, since there is no way of knowing in advance which path leads to the goal state being reached.

The main advantage of the breadth-first search technique is that it provides the solution that takes the fewest moves.

Depth First

In this search technique, each branch of the search tree is searched from top to bottom in turn until either a goal state is found or the end of the branch is reached. If a solution is not reached by the end of a branch, then backtracking takes place to where the last branching decision took place, and the alternative route is searched.

The order of visiting the nodes in the search tree above is:

A, B, F, G, N, O, C, H, D, I, P, J, K, Q, R, E, L, M.

Memory

The depth-first search technique is less memory-intensive than the breadth-first search technique, since, once a search has been made to the end of a branch, then it is no longer required to be stored in memory since it is certain that that branch does not contain the solution.

contd

BREADTH FIRST AND DEPTH FIRST contd

The main advantage of the depth-first search technique is that only the nodes in the current branch being searched have to be held in memory.

Parallel processing is ideally suited to both of these search techniques, since more than one search path can be evaluated simultaneously using several processors, thus speeding up the search time.

COMBINATORIAL EXPLOSION

Using an AI program to play chess better than any human being should simply involve it looking ahead at all the possible moves that could be made and then choosing the ones with the best outcome. However, the number of ways to play the game grows exponentially for each move that is looked ahead, and the number of possibilities soon becomes enormous and unmanageable.

For example, if each move was only a choice of three moves, then looking 20 moves ahead would result in $3^{20} = 3\ 486\ 784\ 401$ possible combinations of moves.

This problem is known as combinatorial explosion.

USE OF HEURISTICS TO REDUCE SEARCH TIME

In some AI problems, the number of combinations of moves is so large that a means is sought to speed up the process of determining the next move.

Heuristics is the process of selecting a smaller number of moves to be searched, based upon the probability that they are better moves. In this way, branches that are not likely to lead to a solution are not examined, and so the search time can be considerably reduced. Heuristics can improve the AI system by performing informed searches that result in reduced search time and smaller demands on memory.

For example, an AI system that determines the shortest route between two towns using the available roads could blindly search through all the possible combinations of roads. The number of searches could be reduced using heuristics to ignore a road that was going away from the target town, since that would be unlikely to provide the best solution.

LET'S THINK ABOUT THIS

Breadth first and depth first are two search techniques that exhaustively search all possible solutions to a problem in turn until a match is made. These search techniques are often asked for in the exam, so make sure that you know how they work and the advantage that each has over the other.

Heuristics is used to reduce the number of searches in an AI problem by using previous knowledge to explore the paths that are more likely to lead to a solution.

DON'T FORGET

Both depth-first and breadth-first searches require backtracking. Depth first can require extensive backtracking when a long branch does not yield a solution. Breadth first can require extensive backtracking when the solution is many horizontal layers in depth.

KNOWLEDGE REPRESENTATION

FEATURES OF A DECLARATIVE LANGUAGE

Recursion

Recursion is a rule whose definition involves the rule itself. The following rule is an example of recursion:

descendant(X, Z) :-descendant(Y, Z), child(X, Y) | X is a descendant of Z IF Y is a descendant of Z AND X is a child of Y.

Negation

Negation reverses logic. It returns FALSE from TRUE and TRUE from FALSE. The number of rules can be reduced by using negation. For example, instead of having a separate rule to define passes and fails in an exam, negation can be used to define passes and then to define fails as people who have NOT passed.

Two rules   **One rule**
passed(person)   passed(person)
failed(person)   NOT passed(person)

Negation can cause a problem if care is not taken in its use. If the knowledge base does not include the fact passed(winston), then NOT passed(winston) would be returned as TRUE. This is due to the fact that passed(winston) is FALSE so that the reverse becomes TRUE.

Inheritance

This works on the principle that, once the facts about a particular group have been entered into a knowledge base, then a member of the group will inherit the characteristics of that group. Inheritance allows fewer rules to be stored in the knowledge base, since members inherit the characteristics of the group.

The example below demonstrates the use of inheritance in a bird knowledge base.

1 has(bird, feathers)
2 has(bird, two legs)
3 has(bird, lays eggs)
4 is_a_bird(eagle)
5 is_a_bird(robin)
6 is_a_bird(penguin)

Rules are defined for the characteristics of a bird. Members of the birds group then inherit the characteristics of birds (feathers, two legs and laying eggs). This saves a lot of memory by not having to define rules for each characteristic for each type of bird.

> Prolog (programming logic) is the declarative language used in this topic to define the facts and rules stored in a knowledge base and to work through a trace for a query. Research Prolog further by entering the keywords 'Prolog' and 'basics' into a search engine.

MANUAL TRACE

A manual trace involves stepping through the lines of a knowledge base, usually using a depth-first search to match a goal, often through matching two or more subgoals.

A knowledge base describing some information on dinosaurs is shown below. Lines 1 to 17 contain facts, and lines 18 and 19 contain rules.

1 eats(brachiosaurus, leaves)   A brachiosaurus eats leaves
2 eats(tyrannosaurus rex, sheep)
3 eats(protoceratops, grass)
4 eats(velociraptor, fruit)
5 eats(velociraptor, cavemen)
6 eats(tyrannosaurus rex, cows)

contd

MANUAL TRACE contd

7 eats(stegosaurus, fruit)
8 eats(albertosaurus, sheep)
9 eats(velociraptor, cows)
10 eats(tyrannosaurus rex, cavemen)
11 eats(brachiosaurus, fruit)
12 animal(sheep)   Sheep are animals
13 animal(cows)
14 animal(cavemen)
15 plant_life(leaves)   Leaves are plant life
16 plant_life(grass)
17 plant_life(fruit)
18 flesheater(X) :- eats(X, Y), animal(Y)   X is a flesh eater if X eats Y AND Y are animals
19 cannibal(X) :- eats(X, X)   X is a cannibal if X eats X

This knowledge base can be interrogated with queries such as ?flesheater(velociraptor). The goal for this query has two subgoals: eats( ) and animal( ). The query requires both of these subgoals to be matched.

The computer system's solution to the query ?flesheater(velociraptor) can be traced manually as follows.

First subgoal eats(velociraptor, Y) is matched at line 4
Y is instantiated to fruit
Second subgoal animal(fruit) fails to make a match
Backtracking to line 5, first subgoal eats(velociraptor, Y) is matched
Y is instantiated to cavemen
Second subgoal animal(cavemen) is matched at line 14
Therefore the result of the query ?flesheater(velociraptor) is TRUE.

Complex query

A complex query requires two or more subgoals to be matched. In the above example, flesheater(X) :- eats(X, Y), animal(Y) is a complex theory but the query cannibal(X) :- eats(X, X) is not.

Instantiation

This term indicates that a search has found an instance of a rule or a fact where a variable has a value.

Backtracking

This means that a solution has not been found in a branch, and the search goes back to where the last decision was made and takes an alternative path in the search for a solution.

DON'T FORGET

The example given here is meant to be representative of what you can expect in the exam. However, this type of question has many variations and twists, so prepare yourself by working through this sort of question in past exam papers.

IMPORTANCE OF THE ORDER OF RULES

It is important to place the rules and facts that are most likely to provide a solution at the beginning of the list in the knowledge base. This provides a faster solution, since fewer matches are required to find a goal.

LET'S THINK ABOUT THIS

The Higher Computing exam always asks a question involving working through a trace similar to the example given in this topic. You should make sure that your answers to these questions refer to line numbers and use the terms **subgoal**, **backtracking** and **instantiation**.

EXAM-STYLE QUESTIONS

DON'T FORGET

These questions are based on the work of the Artificial Intelligence unit. Of course, five questions cannot cover the entire syllabus, and you should make good use of past exam papers for your exam preparation.

QUESTION 1

In the early stages of artificial intelligence, the Turing test was proposed to determine whether a machine can demonstrate true intelligence.

(a) (i) Describe the Turing test.

(ii) Give **two** flaws in the Turing test.

(b) Eliza is a program that allows a computer to simulate a conversation with a human. Give one reason why AI programs such as Eliza do not exhibit real intelligence.

(c) Why has AI been used with great success in game-playing programs such as chess but not so successfully in games such as backgammon?

(4, 1, 1)

QUESTION 2

Computer vision can improve the 'intelligence' of robot arms in a car assembly plant. The first two stages of computer vision are image acquisition and signal processing.

(a) Name and describe the last **three** stages of a computer vision system.

(b) Describe one difficulty the computer vision system may have in identifying a three-dimensional car part from a two-dimensional image.

(c) Describe **two** hardware developments that have contributed to advances in this area of artificial intelligence.

(3, 1, 2)

QUESTION 3

A firm that hires out stretch limousines decides to contract a software development company to develop an expert system to help in the maintenance and repair of its limos.

(a) The software development company uses an expert system shell to implement the software solution. Describe the difference between an expert system and an expert system shell.

(b) Give **one** advantage and **one** disadvantage of using an expert system shell as opposed to an expert system.

(c) The company follows the advice of the expert system and causes irreversible damage to several of the limo engines by pouring in the wrong engine oil.
(i) What are the legal implications in this situation?
(ii) Why might the software development company not be able to be held responsible?

(2, 2, 2)

QUESTION 4

A depth-first or a breadth-first search technique may be used when searching a knowledge base in a declarative language program.

(a) For the search tree shown below, give the order of visiting the nodes in:
  (i)   a breadth-first search
  (ii) a depth-first search.

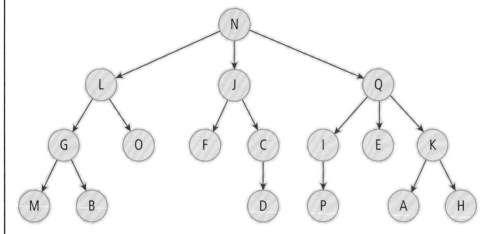

(b) What is meant by the term 'combinatorial explosion' in AI?

(4, 2)

QUESTION 5

Some of the information in the knowledge base of an expert system on fashion models is shown below.

1	is_a(tom, male)	Tom is a male
2	is_a(alan, male)	
3	is_a(claudia, female)	Claudia is a female
4	is_a(rosie, female)	
5	is_a(wendy, female)	
6	junior(tom)	Tom is a junior tennis player
7	junior(rosie)	
8	junior(wendy)	
9	senior(alan)	Alan is a senior tennis player
10	senior(claudia)	
11	girlsteam(X) :- is_a(X, female), junior(X)	X can picked for the girls' team if X is a female AND X is a junior tennis player.

(a) Using an in depth search, trace the first solution to the query
   ?girlsteam (X)

Describe your trace using the terms 'subgoal', 'backtracking' and 'instantiated'.

(b) Explain the term **negation**.

(4, 2)

ARTIFICIAL INTELLIGENCE

ANSWERS

ANSWER 1

2 marks for good explanation

(a) (i) A human communicates with a human and a computer program through terminals. If the human tester can't tell which is the human and which is the computer program, then the computer program has passed the test for artificial intelligence.

2 × 1 mark for each flaw

(ii) The Turing test depends on the intelligence of the interrogator as much as the intelligence of the interrogated human.
The test operates in a restricted domain.

1 mark **(b)** Eliza simply responds to keywords and phrases and shows no adaptability or imagination.

1 mark **(c)** It is hard for the computer to be sure of success because of the random element of throwing dice.

ANSWER 2

1 mark **(a)** Edge detection
The digital data is analysed to produce a simpler outline of the image as defined by its edges.

1 mark Object recognition
Pattern matching is used to identify objects by comparing them with known objects.

1 mark Image understanding
The identified objects are related to each other so that sense can be made of the whole image.

1 mark **(b)** Parts of the car part may be hidden by other objects OR
There may be shadow on the car part OR
The car part may be being viewed from an unusual angle OR
The car part may not be in the known database.

2 × 1 mark for each description

(c) More memory has allowed high resolution and high bit-depth images to be stored.
Faster processors have meant that the graphics data can be manipulated faster.
Parallel processing speeds up the time required to analyse and identify an object.
etc.

ANSWER 3

2 marks **(a)** 2 marks.
Expert system = Explanatory interface + Inference engine + Knowledge base
Expert system shell = Explanatory interface + Inference engine.

1 mark for any one advantage

(b) An expert system is cost-effective, consistent and portable.

1 mark for any one disadvantage

An expert system operates in a narrow domain, lacks common sense, is inflexible and so on.

1 mark **(c) (i)** There is the issue of who is legally responsible for the damage to the car.
1 mark **(ii)** The software development company may have made the user sign a disclaimer.

ANSWER 4

(a) (i)   N, L, J, Q, G, O, F, C, I, E, K, M, B, D, P, A, H.   2 marks

(ii)   N, L, G, M, B, O, J, F, C, D, Q, I, P, E, K, A, H.   2 marks

(b) Combinatorial explosion is where each level of a search tree branches to more nodes so that the number of permutations increases exponentially.   2 marks

ANSWER 5

(a) First subgoal is_a(X, female) is matched at line 3   1 mark
X is instantiated to claudia.
Second subgoal junior(claudia) fails to make a match, so X=claudia is not a solution.   1 mark
Backtracking to line 4, first subgoal is_a(X, female) is matched   1 mark
X is instantiated to rosie.
Second subgoal junior(rosie) is matched at line 7   1 mark
X=rosie is a solution.

(b) Negation is where the opposite logic is returned. TRUE becomes FALSE and FALSE becomes TRUE.   2 marks

NETWORK PROTOCOLS 1

PROTOCOLS

A **protocol** is a set of agreed rules between a sender and receiver so that successful transmission of data can take place. In the context of a computer network, this would involve rules concerning the structure of packets of data, the speed of transmission, the error-checking mechanism being used and so on.

The emergence of standard protocols has contributed to the rapid growth of computer networks and the internet over the last few decades.

DON'T FORGET

The acronym URL can be expanded as Universal Resource Locator as well as Uniform Resource Locator. If the URL of a page is not known, then entering suitable keywords into a search engine can be used to locate the site and other relevant sites.

HTTP (HYPERTEXT TRANSFER PROTOCOL)

HTTP is a protocol used to transfer web pages over the internet.

A Uniform Resource Locator (URL) is used to specify the exact location of the web page on a server.

The URL can be described in several component parts. The URL for a web page about characters in Eastenders on the BBC website is shown below.

http://www.bbc.co.uk/tv/soaps/eastenders/characters.htm

| Protocol | Domain name | Path to page | File name |

TELNET

The Telnet protocol allows a user at a remote computer to log into another computer on the internet and access files on that computer, given that he or she has the appropriate access rights.

For example, someone on a business trip to Las Vegas could use the Telnet protocol to access important files on their home computer. An IP (Internet Protocol) address is used to identify the remote computer. The data is transferred between the two computers in the form of ASCII codes.

FTP (FILE TRANSFER PROTOCOL)

FTP is used to transfer files from one computer to another over the internet. The files can be program or data files. The files are transferred from one computer to another in the form of ASCII codes or binary.

SMTP (SIMPLE MAIL TRANSFER PROTOCOL)

SMTP is used to transfer text-based e-mail messages. The text is transferred in the form of ASCII codes. Attachments such as graphics, sound and video files are encoded into ASCII.

An e-mail address is in the form: a_williams@hotmail.com

OSI (OPEN SYSTEMS INTERCONNECTION) MODEL

The OSI model was developed to allow the wide variety of computers and network software to be able to communicate with each other by using standard protocols.

The OSI model describes the process of transmission of data across a network in seven layers. Each layer is independent of the other layers, so that any changes to one layer will not require changes to the other layers.

contd

OSI (OPEN SYSTEMS INTERCONNECTION) MODEL contd

The Seven Layers of the OSI Model

Layer	Name
1	Physical
2	Data link
3	Network
4	Transport
5	Session
6	Presentation
7	Application

Layer 1
The **Physical layer** is concerned with physical characteristics, i.e. voltage levels for 1 and 0, type of cabling and so on.
Repeaters and hubs operate at this layer, since they are concerned with boosting voltage levels of the bits in packets of data.

Layer 2
The **Data Link layer** is concerned with the size of packets, means of addressing packets, performing error-checking and correction of packets, and so on.
A switch operates at this layer, since it uses the addresses of packets to forward them intelligently in the right direction on a LAN.

Layer 3
The **Network layer** is concerned with routing packets from one network to another over the best path.
A router operates at this layer, since it uses IP addresses to forward packets from one network to another.
The Internet Protocol (IP) operates at this layer.

Layer 4
The **Transport layer** breaks up a file into packets for transmission from one network to another and reassembles them at their destination.
The TCP (Transmission Control Protocol) operates at this layer.

Layer 5
The **Session layer** sets up, manages and terminates communications between two computers.

Layer 6
The **Presentation layer** converts data sent over a network from one type of format to another.
Encryption/decryption and compression/decompression take place here.

Layer 7
The **Application layer** is concerned with techniques that application programs use to communicate with the network, for example Telnet or HTTP.

DON'T FORGET

The IP and TCP protocols are used to transfer data between computers on the internet. These protocols will be described more fully in the next topic.

Look up the website www.cisco.com for a more detailed description of the OSI model. This site also gives lots of other information on network hardware devices and software.

 LET'S THINK ABOUT THIS

HTTP, Telnet, FTP and SMTP are protocols used to transfer data on computer networks.

The OSI model is a seven-layer model describing data transmission on a network. A description of one or two of these layers is commonly asked for in the exam, so learn the concise descriptions given on these pages.

NETWORK PROTOCOLS 2

IP ADDRESSES

Every computer on the internet is identified by an IP address. The IP address is set by the software – unlike a MAC address, which is embedded in the network interface card.

Classes of IP Addresses

The IP address is a 32-bit number made up of four 8-bit parts called octets. Usually the address is displayed not in binary but as four decimal numbers – 172.63.238.106, for example.

The different classes of IP address are achieved by splitting the octets into two parts called the **network identifier** and the **node identifier**. There are three different ways of splitting the address.

Class A	nnn.hhh.hhh.hhh
Class B	nnn.nnn.hhh.hhh
Class C	nnn.nnn.nnn.hhh

n = network identifier
h = node identifier

Class A addresses have their first octet in the range 1 to 126.
Class B addresses have their first octet in the range 128 to 191.
Class C addresses have their first octet in the range 192 to 223.

The network identifier is used to route packets to the destination network. On arrival at the network, the packet is then routed to the individual computer using the node identifier.

Class A: the first octet identifies the company network, and the remaining three octets identify the nodes on that network. This allows for 2^{24} (approx. 16 million) addresses. Class A addresses are used for very large companies.
Class B: the first two octets identify the company network, and the remaining two octets identify the nodes on that network. This allows for 2^{16} (approx. 65 000) addresses. Class B addresses are used for large companies.
Class C: the first three octets identify the company network, and the remaining octet identifies the nodes on that network. This allows for 2^{8} (256) addresses. Class C addresses are used for relatively small networks.

STATIC AND DYNAMIC IP ADDRESSES

DON'T FORGET

Dynamic IP addresses are useful in the situation where there are more computers on the network than IP addresses available to allocate. For example, an ISP (Internet Service Provider) will have more potential customers than it has IP addresses, so it will allocate IP addresses to the subset of customers that are currently logged on.

A static IP address is where the computers are given a fixed IP address that never changes. A dynamic IP address is where the computers on a network are given an IP address when they are connected to the network for that session but which can change each time they are connected.

LIMITATIONS OF IP ADDRESSES

There are 2^{32} (approximately 4,000 million) available IP addresses – and, as the internet continues to expand, these IP addresses are rapidly being used up.

The system for classification of IP addresses is also inefficient, since often all of the allocated addresses in class A and class B addresses are not used.

A solution to the limitations of the IP addressing system is a system called IPV6, which uses 128-bit addresses. This allows for 3.4×10^{38} addresses.

TCP/IP PROTOCOL

The **TCP/IP** protocol is a combination of two protocols which allows computers on different networks to communicate with each other. The computers could be on two LANs in the same building or on two LANs in different countries on the internet.

contd

TCP/IP PROTOCOL contd

When a file is to be transmitted between computers using the TCP/IP protocol, the file is broken up into chunks of data called packets. The TCP/IP protocol operates on packet-switching networks, which means that the packets can take different routes around the network and arrive in any order at their destination.

The TCP (Transmission Control Protocol) inserts a sequence number into each packet so that each packet can be reassembled into the correct order at the destination computer.

The IP (Internet Protocol) inserts the IP address of the destination computer into a header on each packet so that the packets can be forwarded by routers to their destination.

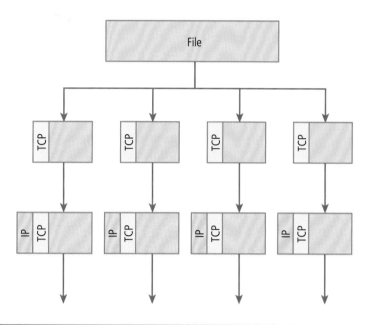

DOMAIN NAMES AND DOMAIN NAME SERVICE (DNS)

A **domain name** is a name used to uniquely define an internet site. The domain name is made up of two or more parts called labels which are separated by dots: for example, www.bbc.co.uk

Some examples of the meaning of domain-name labels are shown in the tables below.

Label	Meaning
.com	Commercial business, a company
.net	Network provider, Internet Service Provider
.edu	Educational institution
.gov	Governmental agency
.org	Non-profit institution
.mil	US military

Label	Country
.uk	United Kingdom
.fr	France
.au	Australia
.jp	Japan
.de	Germany

Domain Name Service (DNS)

Internet sites are identified by **domain names** rather than IP addresses because they are much easier to remember. Domain Name Servers are dedicated servers that keep tables in databases which link domain names to their IP addresses.

Domain Name Resolution is the system of mapping a domain name to its IP address. This is done on the internet by the Domain Name Service performed by Domain Name Servers.

Steps Required for Domain Name Resolution

1 The user types a Domain Name for a website into a browser.
2 A program called a DNS resolver contacts a DNS server, which matches the Domain Name with its IP address.
3 The IP address is sent back to the browser, which can then look up the required website.

LET'S THINK ABOUT THIS

There are three classes of IP address. Class A addresses are for very large organisations, class B for large companies and class C for small networks.

The TCP/IP protocols were developed by ARPANET. Research ARPANET on the internet.

NETWORK APPLICATIONS

BROWSERS AND MICROBROWSERS

A **browser** is a program that is used to locate and display web pages. Most browsers will also have the facility to store frequently visited sites as favourites and also keep a history of pages visited.

Plugins are used to display non-standard (often multimedia) content. Common browsers are Flash, QuickTime and Shockwave.

A **microbrowser** is a program used to locate and display internet content on handheld devices such as mobile phones and PDAs. Microbrowsers offer a smaller-scale version of web pages since these devices operate with lower bandwidth and memory capacity than a desktop computer.

HTML (HYPERTEXT MARKUP LANGUAGE)

HTML is a language used to create web pages. The language uses tags to describe the elements of the page such as a header, title, body, style, font size and so on. A start tag and an end tag are placed around the elements of the page: for example, <.<title>…</title>

The example below shows how tags are used to create a simple HTML document.

```
<html>
<head>
        <title> Higher Computing </title>
</head>
<body>
        <h1> Welcome to the course </h1>
        <p> This text is in normal style </p>
        <p> <b> This text is in bold style </b></p>
        <p> <i> This text is in italic style </i> </p>
        <p align = "center"> This text is centre-aligned </p>
</body>
</html>
```

The <html> tags are placed around the whole file to identify it as an HTML file.

The <head> tag is used at the start of the file to define details such as the title of the page which is defined in the <title> tag.

The <body> tag is placed around the main content of the page.

The <h1> (headline size 1), <p> (new paragraph), <b> (bold), <u> (underline) and <i> (italic) tags are used to format text.

<p align = "center"> is used to centre-align the paragraph text.

Hyperlinks

A hyperlink is implemented by specifying the URL and the text used to activate the link.

For example: <p><a href="http://www.jazzwise.com//">Jazz</a></p>

Research HTML further by entering the keywords 'HTML' and 'tutorial' into a search engine.

WML (WIRELESS MARKUP LANGUAGE)

WML is similar to HTML in that it uses tags to describe the elements of the page such as titles, hyperlinks and text formatting. Since WML documents are downloaded and displayed by small handheld devices, they have limited multimedia support and fewer text-formatting features than HTML documents.

A WML document consists of one or more decks of cards with links to allow the user to navigate between the cards.

contd

WML (WIRELESS MARKUP LANGUAGE) contd

The example below shows how tags are used to create a simple WML document.

```
<wml>
        <card id="welcome">
                <p> Welcome to my WAP site </p>
                <p> <a href ="#higher"> Enter for Higher course details </a> </p>
        </card>
        <card id = "higher">
                <p> Course details: </p>
                <p> Computer Systems </p>
                <p> Software Development </p>
                <p> Optional Topic </p>
                <p> <a href ="#welcome"> Back to welcome card </a> </p>
        </card>
</wml>
```

The elements of the page are defined by start and end tags similar to HTML.
This document has one deck with two cards called "welcome" and "higher".
There are two hyperlinks that allow the user to move between the two cards in the deck.

WAP (Wireless Application Protocol)

The WAP protocol is used for wireless communication between devices such as mobile phones and PDAs (Personal Digital Assistant).

A WAP-enabled phone is one which uses the Wireless Application Protocol to access web content using a micro browser.

DON'T FORGET

WAP is used to retrieve pages written in Wireless Markup Language (WML) just as HTTP is used to retrieve pages written in HTML.

SEARCH ENGINES

Search engines are used to find websites on a specific topic by entering relevant keywords. Google and Ask are examples of search engines. They work by maintaining tables that link websites with keywords.

Meta-tags are put into a web page to provide details about a page that are used by search engines. The most common meta tags are **keywords** and **description**.

The keywords tag is used to list words which describe the content of the page.
The description tag is used to give the text of the summary displayed when the page appears in the results of a search engine.

For example:
```
<meta name="keywords" content="open, open championship, golf, golfcourses"></meta>
<meta name="description" content="The Open Championship Official Website."></meta>
```

Spiders are programs that automatically "crawl" around the web searching for pages to include in search-engine databases. They find the pages by following links in the pages they already have in their database, but also rely on indexing web pages submitted by contributors. The software "crawls" through the web pages using elements such as titles, content, HTML tags and so on to build tables linking pages and their keywords. The pages stored in the search-engine database can then be searched by keyword.

A **meta-search** engine uses several search engines to answer a query and summarises the results. Any duplicates thrown up by the different search engines are removed.

LET'S THINK ABOUT THIS

HTTP documents are transferred over the internet by the HTTP protocol and displayed in a browser. WML documents are transferred over the internet by the WAP protocol and displayed in a microbrowser.

NETWORKS – SOCIAL AND ETHICAL ISSUES

SOCIAL IMPLICATIONS

E-Commerce

This is a term used to describe the buying and selling of goods over the internet. This is a rapidly growing area, although there are still issues of security with credit-card payments and reliability.

Advantages of e-commerce to the customer:

- Goods can be purchased 24/7
- Goods are available from a global market
- Prices can be compared to get the best deal
- Time and money are saved on travelling.

Advantages of e-commerce to the seller:

- No 'middlemen' take any of the profit, since retailers deal directly with the customers
- Customers can be reached anywhere in the world
- There is no need for expensive high-street shops and staff
- EFT (Electronic Funds Transfer) reduces the security problems in handling cash.

Security Measures Against Fraud

Encryption
HTTPS (HTTP over a Secure socket layer) is a protocol to encrypt credit-card data to ensure that it cannot be intercepted when it is being transmitted over the internet.

Artificial Intelligence
AI systems are used to spot unusual card activity, such as very large purchases or sudden increases in transactions, to try to identify the use of stolen card details.

Distance Selling Regulations
Companies selling goods over the internet have to comply with Distance Selling Regulations. These are regulations drawn up to protect the customer.

- Clear information must be provided about the goods or services for sale.
- A confirmation of the purchase must be sent to the customer.
- There is a cooling-off period of seven working days, up to which point the customer can opt out of the sale.

Information-Rich and Information-Poor

People in western countries have access to vast amounts of information on any subject through the internet and other technologies, and are described as information-rich. Most people in the Third World are information-poor in that these countries do not have the expensive equipment and network infrastructure to allow internet access. There is an increasing gulf developing between people who are information-rich and people who are information-poor.

Teleworking

Teleworking is the use of communications technology to work from home some or all of the time.

Advantages of teleworking:

- Time and money are saved on travelling and even on clothes.
- Workers can choose which hours to work to suit themselves.

Disadvantages of teleworking:

- There is a lack of contact with other workers and a feeling of isolation.
- There will be fewer facilities around such as good-quality printers and photocopiers.

contd

SOCIAL IMPLICATIONS contd

Social Isolation

The internet and IT make it possible for people to do tasks from the office or home that could not have been done before without going into town and interacting with other people.

E-commerce means that people use high-street shops less and meet together less as a result. Teleworking means that people work from home instead of in an office with their colleagues. Many people spend hours playing games over the internet and using chatrooms as opposed to going out and socialising with other people.

ETHICAL IMPLICATIONS

Ethical issues related to computer networks include individuals' rights to personal privacy and the censorship of violent and pornographic materials on the internet.

Personal Privacy

Software exists which allows the monitoring of internet and e-mail use by employees. It is now possible to trace the activities and movements of individuals through their use of cash machines, credit-card payments, mobile phones and so on. Some people are worried that governments and employers can collect and use this information against individuals' rights to personal privacy.

Censorship

Legislation is different from country to country, which makes it very difficult to control the information that is available on the internet. Most people would believe that the violent and pornographic materials available on the internet should be removed; but what is considered as acceptable varies around the world in different countries and cultures.

Regulation of Investigatory Powers Act (2000)

This act gives employers the right to monitor e-mails and telephone calls by their employees to make sure that their activities are work-related. Some people consider this act to be an invasion of personal privacy, but others consider that employers should be entitled to make sure that employees in their pay are not wasting time.

Arguments **for** the Regulation of Investigatory Powers Act:

- Businesses should have the right to ensure that their facilities are not being abused.
- Companies need to have a means of identifying employees who are wasting time to the cost of the company.
- It is a government law and therefore needs no justification.

Arguments **against** the Regulation of Investigatory Powers Act:

- Users have the right that personal e-mails should be kept private.
- Users should have the right that all their personal data is kept confidential.
- The act is in opposition to the principles of freedom of speech.

DON'T FORGET

There are **three** other pieces of UK legislation covered in this course:
1 The Data Protection Act
2 The Computer Misuse Act
3 The Copyright, Designs and Patents Act.

These acts were covered in the Standard Grade course but can be required for answering questions in the Higher exam.

 Look up the Regulation of Investigatory Powers Act on the internet for more details about this act.

LET'S THINK ABOUT THIS

Try to talk to a family member or a friend's parent who works from home and ask them about the advantages and disadvantages of teleworking.

The network used in your school will probably have software that allows teachers to monitor the activities of students to make sure that they are not abusing the facilities. Investigate what monitoring software is being used.

NETWORKS – SECURITY AND THREATS

SECURITY MEASURES

Introduction

Different levels of users on a network require different access rights and privileges. For example, a student on a network would not require the same permissions as the network manager who installs new software, changes system settings and so on.

Attacks

Passive attacks involve monitoring and collecting data on a network without the user's knowledge. The data is not altered or changed.

Active attacks involve modifying data on a network, deleting data or deliberately bringing down the network.

Access rights

Users log on to a network by entering a username and a password. The network operating system has a database of information that allocates permissions and access rights to files and folders to the user.

File and Folder Permissions

Read/Write – this allows the user to open the file or folder and save any changes to the file or folder.
Read Only – this allows the user to open the file or folder but not to make any changes.
No Access – this makes the files and folders unavailable to the user.

Access to Hardware

Computers can be physically protected by locking them in secure rooms. Access can be controlled with PIN numbers on locks, iris scans and so on.

The network operating system can be used to restrict particular users' access to particular computers.

NETWORK SECURITY REQUIREMENTS

Confidentiality

It is important that users' data is secure from being viewed or accessed by unauthorised network users or outsiders.

Data Integrity

Data must be transmitted and received without corruption or errors. Error-checking mechanisms such as parity checks and checksums can be used to detect any errors.

Availability

The network should be reliable and robust so that the network users can rely on its services and performance.

DENIAL-OF-SERVICE ATTACKS

A **denial-of-service attack** is when a network server or resources such as hard disc space are put under so much pressure that the network cannot provide its normal services to legitimate users.

contd

DENIAL-OF-SERVICE ATTACKS contd

DoS attacks involve bombarding the network with a high volume of data in a short period of time so that the network can not cope and its operations grind to a halt.

Types of Attack

Bandwidth Consumption

This attack degrades the performance of a server by sending it a large number of data packets in a short period of time. For example, a smurf attack is mounted by sending a packet with a false source address to the broadcast address of a network. (Giving a packet a false source address is called spoofing.) The packet contains a ping message, which is a technique for checking that a communication link is working properly. All of the computers on the network then reply to the ping message, which is actually the address of the target server.

Resource Starvation

An attack can consume other resources apart from bandwidth in order to bring down a server. For example, the server's hard disc space can be used up by sending a large volume of e-mail messages.

Programming Flaw

Software is often released with flaws in the code. This type of attack exploits weaknesses in server software and operating systems.

Routing

This attack involves hi-jacking data packets and routing them to the target server, which gets flooded with data packets, or redirecting packets to a false destination to deny legitimate requests.

DNS

In this attack, a large number of DNS queries with a spoofed IP address of the target server are sent to a DNS server. The DNS server then floods the target server with an excessive number of replies.

Reasons for Attacks

There are several reasons why DoS attacks are carried out.

Malicious

Individuals think that it is good fun to bring down an organisation's network.

Personal

Disgruntled employees who bear a grudge can see a DoS attack as revenge against their employer.

Political

Sometimes, DoS attacks can be politically motivated, such as an attack on a government network or to bring down a rival company in business.

Costs of Attacks

A DoS attack can be very costly to an organisation for several reasons.

1 the loss of business during the attack downtime
2 the cost of repair and response to the attack
3 loss of confidence by users in the organisation.
4 disruption to the organisation.

DON'T FORGET

It is a common mistake to state that a DoS attack is brought about by flooding a server with a vast amount of data but not mentioning that it is in a short period of time. It is the fact that the server can't deal with a large volume of data in a short period of time that brings it down.

LET'S THINK ABOUT THIS

Pinging is a diagnostic test used to check if an Internet link is working. Find out more about how to send ping messages.

There are several methods and reasons for mounting Denial of Service attacks which can be very costly to an organisation.

NETWORK PROTECTION

INTERNET FILTERING SOFTWARE

Firewall

Firewalls are used by organisations that are concerned with issues of security to filter Internet traffic.

A firewall may be used by employers to prevent employees from wasting time in surfing the net for their own entertainment or by parents or educational institutions to protect children from unsuitable Internet material.

Functions of firewalls include:

1 IP address-filtering, permitting only selected IP addresses access to a local-area network from the internet and vice versa

2 preventing computer ports from being accessed by Trojans

3 stateful packet inspection, where the firewall scans for problems in a packet that could be associated with a DoS attack.

Walled Garden

This is used in educational establishments to provide a limited safe area of the Internet to children.

DON'T FORGET

The proxy server is identified on the internet by an IP address, but the other computers on the LAN don't require an IP address and can use any protocol to send and receive data from the proxy server.

Functions of a walled garden include:

1 restricting access to websites that have been approved by the ISP

2 filtering keywords to deny access to inappropriate websites.

Proxy Server

A proxy server is a computer that is used as a single point of contact between a LAN and the Internet. It can be used to run a firewall to filter unwanted material and is commonly used to cache web pages to make these pages immediately available to other network users.

DISASTER AVOIDANCE

Regular Maintenance

Using good-quality components and having regular maintenance checks can help to avoid failure of hardware components.

Anti-virus Software

The installation of anti-virus software on the server and workstations can help to protect a network against virus threats. It is important that the anti-virus software is regularly updated because new viruses are being created all the time.

contd

DISASTER AVOIDANCE contd

Fault-Tolerance Components

This simply means duplicating hardware components so that the duplicate can take over if a device fails. Equipment such as servers, routers and switches can be duplicated and configured with the same software and data as the original devices so that they can be immediately replaced.

Uninterrupted Power Supply (UPS)

This is a device that supplies enough electricity to a server to keep it functioning during a power cut. The electricity is supplied by a battery or in a larger organisation by a generator. An UPS can also be used to smooth out erratic power supplies whose fluctuations can cause damage to a server.

BACKUP STRATEGIES

Backup Server

Some systems have a backup server that has the configuration and software of the network server in place so that the backup server can replace the network server immediately in the event of failure.

RAID (Random Array of Inexpensive Discs)

A RAID system involves the server duplicating network data to a series of inexpensive discs. This allows the reinstallation of the data on a failed disc from the RAID discs to be done 'live' without the need to shut down the system.

 Explore RAID systems further by entering the keywords 'RAID' and 'discs' into a search engine.

DON'T FORGET

RAID systems can use inexpensive discs for the duplicated data since this is not the live data but simply a precautionary backup of the data that can be made live in case of failure of the normal working discs.

Mirror Discs

This is the act of writing data to two discs simultaneously so that, in the event of failure of one disc, the other can be used instantly.

Tape

Backups used to be kept on magnetic tape because the tapes are cheap and portable. The advent of inexpensive high capacity optical discs such as CD R/W and DVD R/W are now being used more frequently for backups.

Backup Schedule

Loss of data can be catastrophic to an organisation. For example a bank would be in serious trouble if it lost millions of customer records.

It is therefore important that an organisation has a backup strategy that minimises loss of data in the event of a disaster such as a virus attack or sabotage by a disgruntled employee.

Usually a daily backup tape is rotated every five days with an additional weekly backup every four weeks so that data can be recovered from up to a month earlier.

The backup tapes are often taken to another site to increase the chances of recovery in the advent of disasters such as fire or earthquakes which might destroy the backup tapes.

LET'S THINK ABOUT THIS

Explore the security of your school network by finding out what security is being offered by firewalls and walled gardens.

The network manager in your school will have a strategy to backup the data on the network. Find out what backing store device is used to store the backup data and what schedule is used for the backups.

DATA TRANSMISSION AND NETWORK SWITCHING 1

SYNCHRONOUS AND ASYNCHRONOUS TRANSMISSION

Asynchronous Transmission

In asynchronous data transmission (the sender and receiver are not synchronised), the sender sends only one character at a time. Each character is delimited by a start bit and one or more stop bits. There may be a period of idle time between the transmission of characters.

	Data						Data		
1 1	0 1 1 1 0 0 0 1	0		Idle time		1 1	0 1 1 1 0 0 0 1	0

2 stop bits   1 start bit   2 stop bits   1 start bit

Asynchronous transmission is a basic method of data transmission and is only suitable for sending a small amount of data. The extra padding of the start and stop bits makes it a slow and inefficient method. It is, however, an inexpensive method of data transmission that is suitable for low-speed transmission.

Synchronous Transmission

In synchronous data transmission (the sender and receiver are synchronised), the sender sends a packet of data at a time. Synchronisation is achieved by the sender sending a start frame to the receiver to signal that a packet of data is about to be sent and a stop frame to signal the end of transmission.

Stop frame	Data up to 8K	Start frame

Synchronous transmission is a more efficient method of data transmission than asynchronous transmission, since a start and stop frame is only required at the beginning and end of each packet whereas asynchronous data transmission requires start and stop bits with each byte.

ERROR-CHECKING

If an error is detected during transmission, then the receiver sends a signal to the sender to re-transmit the data. In asynchronous data transmission, only the byte with the error has to be sent again, but in synchronous transmission the whole block with the error has to be re-sent.

Parity check

In asynchronous transmission, a parity check can be used to detect any errors in each character being sent. (The details of how a parity check operates were dealt with in the topic "Data Representation 2".)

Checksum

In synchronous transmission, a checksum can be used to detect errors in each block of data being sent. The checksum is generated by treating each byte as a number and adding up all of the bytes in the block.

DON'T FORGET

A parity check is used to detect errors in a single byte whereas a checksum and a cyclic redundancy check are used to detect errors in a block of data.

| 00110100 | 11011001 | 01000001 | .... | 01100101 | 01000001 | Checksum |

Block of data

The checksum is attached to the block and transmitted along with the block of data.

The receiver performs the same calculation and checks to see if its own checksum agrees with the sent checksum. If the re-calculated checksum does not agree with the sent checksum, then the receiver sends a signal to the sender to re-transmit the block of data.

Cyclic Redundancy Check (CRC)

The block of data is treated as a single binary number which is divided by an integer that is agreed between the sender and receiver. The remainder from the calculation is appended to the block of data and transmitted with it. The receiving device does the same calculation and checks that it agrees with the sent remainder. If the values are not the same, then a signal is sent to the sender to transmit the block of data again.

 Research cyclic redundancy checks further by entering 'CRC' into a search engine.

LET'S THINK ABOUT THIS

Asynchronous transmission sends one character at a time with a parity check to detect errors. Synchronous transmission sends a block of data at a time with a checksum to detect errors.

There is a degree of overlap between the work covered in the mandatory Computer Systems chapter in the Networking 1 and Networking 2 pages and the work covered in this optional Computer Networking chapter. It is essential that you learn the basics in the Computer Systems chapter to give yourself a foundation before tackling the work in this chapter.

DATA TRANSMISSION AND NETWORK SWITCHING 2

CSMA/CD (CARRIER SENSE MULTIPLE ACCESS COLLISION DETECTION)

Ethernet

Ethernet is a shared-media bus network where all computers share a common bus for data transmission. The nodes are in competition for access since only one computer can transmit on the bus at one time.

 Explore the Ethernet bus network further by entering the keywords 'Wikipedia' and 'Ethernet' into a search engine. Investigate features of an Ethernet network such as bandwidth, hardware devices and transmission media.

CSMA/CD is a control protocol used to manage the transmissions on the shared bus and minimise collisions occurring by two computers attempting to transmit at the same time.

Ethernet Frame

Data is transmitted in frames (packets) which contain the destination address, the source address, the data itself, error-detection information and some additional information necessary for successful transmission. The computers on the Ethernet network are identified by a MAC address embedded in the NIC. Small frames where there is not much data are given some 'padding' to make it easier for the system to detect collisions. A checksum is used to detect any errors in transmission.

8 bytes	6 bytes	6 bytes	46 to 1500 bytes	4 bytes
Preamble	Source Address	Destination Address	Data	Checksum

CS (Carrier Sense)

This is used to stop computers from attempting to transmit on the common bus when it is being used by another computer and to prevent collisions from occurring. The computers listen to detect if there is any network traffic before they attempt to transmit on the common bus. If one computer is transmitting, then the other computers will refrain from transmitting until the main bus is free.

MA (Multiple Access)

This means that all the computers on the network have equal rights to transmit. No computer has priority over any another computer.

CD (Collision Detection)

The situation can arise where a computer is transmitting on the bus and two other computers are waiting to transmit. When the bus becomes free, the two other computers transmit at the same time and a collision occurs. The computers can detect the collision, and transmission stops. The network operating system then gives each computer a short random period of time to wait before attempting to re-transmit.

On a network with a high volume of data transmissions, delays for computers waiting to transmit can reduce network performance.

 Explore the CSMA/CD control protocol further by entering 'CSMA/CD' into a search engine.

DON'T FORGET

The analogies of 'Listen before talking' and 'Listen while talking' are often used to describe the CS (Carrier Sense) and CD (Collision Detection) protocols.

NETWORK SWITCHING

Circuit Switching

A circuit is connected between the sender and the receiver before transmission takes place and is maintained throughout the transmission.

All of the data follows the same path between the sender and the receiver.

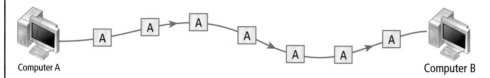

Advantages
The transfer is fast since the connection is not shared with other transmissions.
Packets do not need to be reassembled since they arrive one after another.

Disadvantages
No other computers can transmit over the connection until the transmission is completed.
It is usually expensive since it requires a dedicated connection.

Packet Switching

The data to be transmitted is broken up into blocks of data called packets. These packets are given a destination address and a sequence number, and this information is required to reassemble the packets when they arrive at their destination since the packets may follow different routes between the transmitter and the receiver.

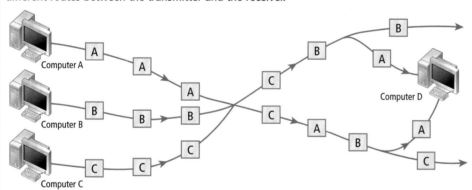

Advantages
Packet switching is usually much cheaper than circuit switching because it does not need a dedicated connection.

Communications channels can be shared since packets from different users can be mixed along a transmission line.

Disadvantages
The transfer is slow compared to circuit switching since the connection is shared with other data.
Packets need to be reassembled at the destination.

DON'T FORGET

The internet uses packet switching to transmit data on a global network of interconnected computer networks and individual computers.

LET'S THINK ABOUT THIS

CSMA/CD is a network protocol used on an Ethernet network to manage the data transmissions on a shared bus.

Circuit switching and packet switching are two techniques used to transmit data on networks. In circuit switching, the entire data follows the same path. In packet switching, the data is broken into packets, each of which can take a different route to the destination where the packets are reassembled.

WIRELESS NETWORKING

INTRODUCTION

Wireless networks use radio waves instead of cables to transmit data between computers.

The wireless technology ranges from transmitting data over a few metres to a printer to accessing information globally on the internet. Wireless technologies remove the hassle of cable-connected devices in a less cluttered environment. The importance to people of staying connected to the internet has seen the technology grow to a point where wireless internet has become available with a Wi-Fi connection in airports, hotels and coffee shops.

The growth of wireless networking is becoming more and more evident in homes, where families are increasingly connecting two or more computers to the internet through a wireless router. There is a compromise with the speed of the connection, but the convenience of being able to move from room to room makes this more than justifiable in most cases.

The prevalence of wireless technologies is certain to continue to grow as the technology improves and issues of transmission speed and security are overcome.

Wireless communication is typically slower than a wired connection, and has issues of security since it is relatively easy to tap into the transmissions. There have also been concerns that the radiation emitted by wireless devices such as mobile phones could be a long-term health hazard to the user.

Look at the website www.pcworld.co.uk to research the variety of wireless devices that are available. Investigate the characteristics and prices of devices such as wireless keyboards, mice, routers and so on.

DON'T FORGET

Bluetooth devices use radio waves for data transmission, so they do not have to be in line of sight of each other and can even be in other rooms in a building.

WPAN (WIRELESS PERSONAL AREA NETWORK)

This is a network that uses wireless transmissions to connect all the devices used by an individual person. A **WPAN** could be used to connect up devices such as laptops, printers, mobile phones and PDAs (Personal Digital Assistant).

Bluetooth is a low-bandwidth wireless technology used over short distances (typically up to 10 metres). It is used to transmit data between devices in a WPAN such as mobile phones, headphones, wireless mice, printers and so on. Each Bluetooth device is identified with a 48-bit address which allows for 2^{48} (approx. 250 000 billion) addresses.

WLAN (WIRELESS LOCAL AREA NETWORK)

This is a LAN where conventional cables and network interface cards have been replaced with wireless connections and wireless network interface cards.

Wireless LANs have a lower **bandwidth** than conventional LANs, with typical speeds of around 20 Mbps for a wireless LAN against 100 Mbps for a LAN with cabling.

The clients on a WLAN are fitted with a wireless network card which communicates with a wireless hub, which in turn is linked to a server.

Advantages of a WLAN

Portable computers such as laptops can be freely moved around the workplace.
There is no need for cabling, which can be expensive or difficult to install.
There is a clutter-free environment with less chance of accidents and fire occurring.

Disadvantages of a WLAN

Security is a concern, since it is harder to check which computers are connected to the network than with cabled computers. Wireless networks use encryption to ensure that useful information cannot be extracted from intercepted transmissions.

WWAN (WIRELESS WIDE AREA NETWORK)

This is a WAN where the traditional links of telecommunications cables have been replaced with wireless connections.

The wireless links can be achieved in several ways:

1 A low-speed solution is to use a mobile phone to connect a laptop to the telephone system. However, this is slow and expensive and not practical for sending anything other than small amounts of data.

2 A satellite link is a better solution but is also very expensive and will only work where a satellite can be accessed.

3 Wireless broadband does not offer the mobility of the other two solutions but is less expensive. Wireless broadband uses a hub to send and receive data to and from transceivers which are mounted on buildings that require access to the WAN. The transmissions are amplified and forwarded between buildings using repeaters.

DON'T FORGET

A transceiver is so called because it is a device that sends and receives data transmissions.

LET'S THINK ABOUT THIS

The Higher coursework task is increasingly demanding knowledge of wireless devices to reflect the changes taking place from cabled to wireless technologies. Use computing literature and the internet to keep up with these developments.

There are a large number of abbreviations and acronyms in the Higher Computing course. When asked to describe a term such as 'WPAN', it is not enough just to expand the acronym. It is certainly a good idea to give the expansion in your answer but also to give a description of the term.

INTERNET CONNECTIONS

BANDWIDTH

Bandwidth is the speed at which data is transmitted over a network, usually measured in bits per second. The **bit** is the unit for measuring the quantity of data transmitted, and transmission speed is measured in megabits per second (Mbps) or kilobits per second (Kbps).

Unit	Transmission speed
1 Kbps	1024 bits per second
1 Mbps	1 048 576 bits per second

DIALUP

This is a connection that provides internet access via the public telephone line through the services of an ISP (Internet Service Provider).

The connection uses a modem to send and receive data to and from the internet. The modem converts the digital signal from the computer to an analogue signal that can be sent down a telephone line and performs the opposite process on incoming data.

A dialup session starts by a password being authenticated followed by a time delay while a connection is made with the ISP.

A protocol called PPP (Point-to-Point Protocol) is used to allow IP packets to be transmitted with a modem over the telephone line.

Advantages
It is a relatively inexpensive connection.

Disadvantages
Dialup has a bandwidth of 56 Kbps, which is very slow by today's standards.

The connection is not always on, so there is a time delay at the start of each session while the connection is established.

ISDN (INTEGRATED SERVICE DIGITAL NETWORK)

This connection transmits digital data over traditional telephone lines. Since the transmission is digital, it can provide a higher bandwidth and more reliable connection than a dialup connection. ISDN lines can be grouped together to offer bandwidths in multiples of 128 Kbps per line but can be costly, as each line is charged separately.

The ISDN line does not use a modem but uses a device called an ISDN terminal adapter to send and receive data to and from the telephone line.

Advantages
There is a reasonably high bandwidth.
There is a very short connection time.

Disadvantages
It can be expensive if many lines are combined to achieve a high bandwidth.

BROADBAND

This internet connection offers a much faster bandwidth than those using traditional telephone connections. This is because **broadband** uses cables that are capable of carrying multiple streams of data simultaneously. This allows the transmission of voice, data and video signals over a single medium. Cable television uses broadband techniques to deliver dozens of channels over one cable.

Broadband speeds have a bandwidth of the order of several Mbps.

 Use the internet to look up currently available broadband speeds from companies such as BT and Virgin Media by entering the keywords 'broadband' and 'deal' into a search engine.

Advantages
There is a very high bandwidth.
The connection is always on, so there is no waiting time at the start of a session.

Disadvantages
It is an expensive connection, especially for the highest bandwidths.

 **DON'T FORGET**

Home users with a broadband connection can use the telephone and surf the internet at the same time. This is not possible with a dialup connection because the line can only carry one signal at a time.

LEASED LINE

Companies pay for the use of a leased line to connect two locations and avoid competition for the bandwidth of public communications channels. It allows a company to have a dedicated line and guarantee the full use of its bandwidth for their own network transmissions.

A leased line is called a T1 connection and can supply a bandwidth of 1.544 Mbps.

Advantages
There is no competition for bandwidth.
There is good security, since it is only used by the company paying for the leased line.

Disadvantages
It can be expensive to set up and maintain the line.

DON'T FORGET

A leased line is sometimes called a Symmetric Digital Subscriber Line (SDSL) (to distinguish it from ADSL).

ADSL (ASYMMETRIC DIGITAL SUBSCRIBER LINE)

An **ADSL** connection is similar to leased lines in that a link must be configured to connect two distinct places. ADSL provides download speeds of up to 9 Mbps and upload speeds of up to 640 Kbps.

ADSL is suited to the home user, who usually requires a fast download speed but not usually a fast upload speed.

ADSL is described as asymmetric because it has different download and upload speeds.

Advantages
There is a high bandwidth for downloading data.
The connection is always on.

Disadvantages
There is a low bandwidth for uploading data.

LET'S THINK ABOUT THIS

Types of internet connections can be evaluated by characteristics that include bandwidth, cost and whether they are always on or not.

High-bandwidth broadband has been allowed by advances in transmission media such as optical fibres and wireless transmissions. Use computer literature and the internet to research the transmission media used in broadband technology.

COMPUTER NETWORKING

EXAM-STYLE QUESTIONS

DON'T FORGET

These questions are based on the work of the Computer Networking unit. Of course, five questions cannot cover the entire syllabus, and you should make good use of past exam papers for your exam preparation.

QUESTION 1

Wendy is on holiday in Australia visiting her goddaughter Polly. She wants to access files on her computer in the UK to show Polly pictures of her pet poodle. Wendy has heard of a protocol that is used on the internet that would allow her to do his.

(a) (i) What is meant by the term protocol?

(ii) **Name** a protocol that would allow her to access her home computer from abroad.

(b) Describe the structure of a URL address by using the example below.
http://www.showdogs.com/poodles/features/grooming.htm

(2, 4)

QUESTION 2

IP addresses are in the form of 32-bit numbers made up of four octets.

Different classes of IP address are achieved by splitting the octets into two parts in different ways.

(a) (i) Describe how the octets in a class B address are used to indicate the network and the node.

(ii) Give **two** limitations of the current IP addressing system.

(b) (i) Why is the Domain Name Service required if computers on the internet can be identified by their IP address?

(ii) Describe the process of Domain Name Resolution.

(3, 3)

QUESTION 3

Winston has used WML to write web content for a company providing an online sports results service. His manager wants him to write similar web pages in HTML.

(a) Describe **one** similarity and **one** difference between WML and HTML.

(b) Why would Winston's manager want to create the web content in HTML as well as WML?

(c) Winston's employer is suspicious that some of his employees are wasting time sending e-mails to their friends instead of doing their work.
(i) **Name** a legal act that employers can use to make sure that their employees' activities are work-related.
(ii) Give **one** argument for and **one** argument against this act.

(2, 1, 3)

QUESTION 4

Wendy Wyper works as a network manager for the New Zealand government defence department. She is responsible for the network security. Wendy is concerned that the network is not fully protected against a DoS attack.

(a) Explain what is meant by a DoS attack, and give a means of preventing it from happening.

(b) The network has a bus topology that uses the CSMA/CD protocol. Describe the operation of CSMA/CD.

(3, 3)

QUESTION 5

A mobile-phone company has 18 offices throughout Scotland which are linked in a WAN. Throughout the day, sales information is transmitted over the WAN.

(a) Each month, the company director sends a spreadsheet file to branch managers giving summaries of the month's sales. The network has a bandwidth of 2.75 Mbps, and the file size of the spreadsheet is 885 Kb.

Calculate how long it would take to transmit this file.

(b) The company has set up a website where it sells its products online.
    (i)   Describe **two** benefits to the company of selling goods online.
    (ii) Give **one** method of improving the security of online selling.

(3, 3)

COMPUTER NETWORKING

ANSWERS

ANSWER 1

1 mark   **(a) (i)**   A set of rules of communication agreed between a sender and receiver.

1 mark   **(ii)**   Telnet.

4 × 1 mark for   **(b)**   http – Hypertext transfer protocol (a protocol used to transfer web pages over the internet).
description of   www.showdogs.com – the domain name.
each part   /poodles/features/ – the path to the page.
                        grooming.htm – the file name.

ANSWER 2

1 mark   **(a) (i)**   In a class B address, the first two octets are the network identifier and the last two octets are the node identifier.

2 × 1 mark for each   **(ii)**   There are 2^{32} (approximately 4,000 million) available IP addresses, which are quickly
limitation   being used up as the Internet continues to grow.
                        The system for classification of IP addresses is inefficient, since all of the allocated
                        addresses in class A and class B addresses are often not used.

1 mark   **(b) (i)**   Domain names are much easier to remember than IP addresses.

2 marks   **(ii)**   Domain Name Resolution is the system of mapping a domain name to its IP address.
                        This is done on the internet by Domain Name Servers, which keep tables linking
                        domain names with IP addresses.

ANSWER 3

1 mark for similarity   **(a)**   WML and HTML both use tags to describe elements of the document such as Titles and
                      Text formatting.

1 mark for difference   WML has limited multimedia support and fewer text-formatting features than HTML.

1 mark   **(b)**   Creating the document in HTML would allow it to be made available on the internet and
                     displayed in browsers running on a desktop computer.

1 mark   **(c) (i)**   Regulation of Investigatory Powers Act (2000).

1 mark for an argument   **(ii)**   Businesses should have the right to ensure that their facilities are not
for the act   being abused.

1 mark for an argument   Users should have the right that all their personal data is kept private.
against the act

ANSWER 4

(a) A DoS (Denial of Service) attack is when a network server or resources such as hard disc space are put under so much pressure that the network cannot provide its normal services to legitimate users.

2 marks for the description

DoS attacks can be prevented by installing firewalls to monitor incoming and outgoing traffic and up-to-date anti-virus software.

1 mark for a means of prevention

(b) CSMA/CD consists of:

3 × 1 mark

CS (Carrier Sense), which means that computers can sense if the bus is free before attempting to transmit.

MA (Multiple Access), which means that each computer has equal rights to transmit.

CD (Collision Detection), which means that computers can detect a collision if two or more computers attempt to transmit simultaneously when the bus becomes free.

ANSWER 5

(a) The file size in bits = $885 \times 1024 \times 8 = 7\,249\,920$ bits
Bandwidth = $2.75 \times 1\,048\,576 = 2\,883\,584$ bits per second
Transmission time = $7\,249\,920 / 2\,883\,584 = $ **2.51 seconds**.

3 × 1 mark for each line of calculation

(b) (i) Customers can be reached worldwide.
There is no need for expensive high-street shops and staff, and so on.

2 × 1 mark for each benefit

(ii) HTTPS (HTTP over a Secure socket layer) can be used, which is a protocol that encrypts credit-card data transmitted over the internet.

1 mark

THE DEVELOPMENT PROCESS

THE STAGES IN THE DEVELOPMENT OF A MULTIMEDIA APPLICATION

DON'T FORGET

The production of a multimedia application or a website progresses through the same seven stages that you met earlier in the Software Development unit.

Analysis

At this stage, the requirements of the client are identified and a requirements specification for the project is produced. This will be done through techniques such as interviewing, questionnaires and so on.

Design

At this stage, the screen layouts of the multimedia application or web pages are determined. The most common technique for this is **storyboarding**, which contains details of the multimedia elements of each screen and their layout, specifies links between screens and so on.

Implementation

At this stage, the multimedia application or website is created, usually with an authoring package.

Testing

The following techniques can be used to test the project to locate and remove any errors.

1 Check that video and sound elements play properly.
2 Try out all the links between screens.
3 Perform beta testing, where the clients try out the software in their own workplace.

Documentation

A user guide and a technical guide will be produced at this stage to assist the clients in the use of the software and to support technical staff in its maintenance.

Evaluation

A checklist of criteria will be produced to judge to what extent the product meets the requirements specification.

Maintenance

At some point in the future, the software may require to be modified to remove previously undetected errors, to meet new client requirements or to incorporate improved changes in multimedia technology.

CREATION OF MULTIMEDIA APPLICATIONS AND WEB PAGES

Multimedia Applications

Presentation Software
A presentation package is used to create a sequence of screens which are displayed in a slide show. The slides include the multimedia elements of text, graphics, video and sound. The order of the slides can be linear, or hyperlinks can be used to navigate around the slides.

Authoring Software
An authoring package is used to create an interactive stand-alone multimedia application. Programming code can be incorporated to control how the multimedia elements respond to the user's input.

contd

CREATION OF MULTIMEDIA APPLICATIONS AND WEB PAGES contd

Web Pages

Text Editors

Web pages can be created by entering HTML code into a text editor. This is time-consuming and requires a lot of technical knowledge of HTML. However, this method does allow the web-page author to have more versatility and control over the layout and features of the web page. Viewing the HTML document requires it to be saved and opened in a suitable browser.

WYSIWYG Editors (What You See Is What You Get)

Using WYSIWYG editors allows for simpler entering, formatting and editing of multimedia elements. The elements are simply dragged and dropped onto the page and formatted from menu choices. The results are seen immediately on screen as the elements are created and amended. Most WYSIWYG editors also have a preview option that allows you to see how the web pages will look in a browser as the development proceeds.

However, WYSIWYG editors are limited to the functions available in the package, whereas an expert in HTML code could use a text editor to gain greater control over customisation of the web page.

Find out more about Dreamweaver, which is an application widely used commercially to produce websites. You can find information on the Adobe website (www.adobe.com).

STREAMING OF MULTIMEDIA DATA AND EMBEDDED FILES

In **streaming** , when some of the transmitted data arrives at the computer or device, the multimedia file begins to play while the remainder is still being downloaded. Streaming of data requires the following steps:

1 The data is compressed by the server computer to speed up transmission time.
2 The data is sent in packets to the destination computer.
3 The packets are decompressed by the destination computer as they arrive.
4 The data is passed to a video or sound card for processing and digital-to-analogue conversion.
5 A few seconds of the processed data is placed in a buffer and played as the next parts of the streamed data continue to arrive.

Instead of streaming data, it can be inserted as part of the web page itself as an **embedded file** . This removes the need to stream the data but can substantially increase the size of the file and increase the time to download it.

CODEC AND CONTAINER FILES

Codec

The term 'codec' comes from the words 'compressor' and 'decompressor'. Files are compressed, particularly in multimedia where the file sizes are large, to save on storage space and allow faster transmission across computer networks. The compression and decompression is usually performed by software, but there are hardware-based codec systems that use specially designed microprocessors.

Container Files

Sometimes, several files may require to be grouped for storage or transmission across a computer network. A container file is used to hold a variety of files in one compressed file. This is more convenient than storing or transmitting each compressed file independently.

LET'S THINK ABOUT THIS

Plugins help your browser perform specific functions like viewing special graphic formats or playing multimedia files. Find out about plugins that are commonly used with web pages. Open any web page in Internet Explorer and choose Source on the View menu to look at the HTML code for the page.

BIT-MAPPED GRAPHICS DATA

HARDWARE USED TO CAPTURE STILL GRAPHICS

CCD (Charged Coupled Device)

Digital cameras and scanners use an assembly of charge coupled devices (CCD) – a series of photo sensors that detect the light from an image and convert it into an analogue voltage.

ADC (Analogue-to-Digital Conversion)

The analogue voltages representing the colour of each pixel are converted into digital data to represent each pixel in the image.

Digital Camera and Scanner

A **digital camera** camera uses a two-dimensional array of CCD sensors with each CCD capturing the data for one pixel. A typical digital camera can capture around 9 megapixels. The images are usually stored on a memory card, which can have a capacity of several gigabytes. A **scanner** uses a row of CCD sensors (linear CCD) that moves across the width of a document capturing rows of pixels as it moves.

COMPRESSION TECHNIQUES AND FILE FORMATS

Compression Techniques

RLE (Run Length Encoding)
Often, an image has areas where the same coloured pixel is repeated many times. This technique stores the colour code for 1 pixel and how many times it is repeated instead of the same code over and over again. This can reduce the file size considerably if large areas are the same colour.

LZW (Lempel Ziv Welch)
This compression technique looks for commonly repeated patterns of bits that are then stored in a look-up table. Each pattern is allocated an index number so that the index number can be stored rather than the patterns.

CLUT (Colour Look-up Table)
This is a facility that enables a subset of colours to be stored as a local palette. For example, an 8-bit code would give a CLUT with 256 colours, which could be selected from a full 24-bit colour range. This gives the user control over the specific colours used in a document.

File Formats

24-bit bit-mapped graphics give true colour with 2^{24} colours but are heavy on storage requirements. RLE and LZW compression can be used to reduce the file size.

GIF (Graphics Interchange Format)
GIF uses LZW lossless compression. Each pixel is represented in 8 bits, which allows for 256 colours.

GIF images can be interlaced to create a special visual effect. With an interlaced image, the image looks blurry at first and then comes gradually into focus while the drawing of the image is completed. Without interlacing, the picture fills in slowly line by line from top to bottom. GIFs have a transparency feature where a specific colour can be made transparent so that parts of an image do not obscure the one behind, as shown alongside.

Animated GIFs create apparent movement by showing a sequence of still frames. A rate of around 20 frames per second is needed to produce reasonably fluent motion, so file sizes can be large. LZW compression is commonly used to reduce the file size of animated GIF files.

PNG (Portable Network Graphics)
This is a lossless file format intended to replace GIF by adding extra features. The PNG file format has a higher compression factor than GIF files and also has a transparency feature, but in addition it has an opaqueness attribute that sets the degree of transparency of pixels.

DON'T FORGET

The calculations in this topic are covered in the Computer Systems unit, but in the Multimedia Technology unit you can be asked to do more complex calculations such as working out the bit depth from the file size and resolution.

contd

COMPRESSION TECHNIQUES AND FILE FORMATS contd

JPEG (Joint Photographic Expert Group)
This file format uses 'lossy' compression. The loss in detail can range from being barely noticeable to seriously reducing the quality of the image.

RGB COLOUR CODES

This is a system for representing colours in a computer system using a combination of the three primary colours red, green and blue. RGB typically uses 24 bits to represent a colour by specifying the amount of each colour in 8 bits.

RGB(255, 255, 0) represents 'Yellow' since a combination of red and green produces yellow.
RGB(255, 105, 180) represents 'Hot pink' since it is mainly red with some green and blue.

Look up RGB colour charts by entering the keywords 'RGB' and 'chart' into a search engine.

CALCULATION OF BIT DEPTH

Calculate the bit depth of the image on the right, which has a 720 × 240 resolution and a file size of 337.5 Kb.

Number of bits = 337.5 × 1024 × 8 = 2 764 800 bits
Number of pixels = 720 × 240 = 172 800 pixels
Bit depth = 2 764 800 / 172 800 = 16 bits

240 pixels

720 pixels

DITHERING, ANTI-ALIASING AND INCREASED RESOLUTION

Dithering

This is a technique that tricks the eye into seeing colours that cannot be represented, by placing different-coloured pixels in blocks of colour. This is because the human eye tends to blur adjacent colours together and merge them into a single shade of colour.

Anti-aliasing

Aliasing is where a line or a curve is displayed with a jagged edge, usually due to low resolution. Anti-aliasing smooths out the line by changing the shading, size or alignment of some of the pixels.

Increased Resolution

The image may be required to be resampled by rescanning at a higher resolution to give finer detail and reduce the jagged appearance of the image. This of course will increase the file size.

GRAPHICS CARDS

A **graphics card** manages the display on the monitor. It is a circuit board with its own processor and memory which is used to take some pressure off the computer's main processor and memory. A graphics card has the following features:

1 a DSP (Digital Signal Processor) to allow hardware decoding of graphics data
2 additional RAM to store the graphics data
3 ADC (Analogue-to-Digital Conversion) to convert analogue data to digital for input
4 DAC (Digital-to-Analogue Conversion) to convert digital data.

GPU

Graphics cards have a GPU (Graphics Processing Unit), which is a processor that performs tasks specifically for 3-D graphics. The GPU carries out the intensive processing required to perform such functions as repositioning, rescaling and resizing complex 3-D objects.

LET'S THINK ABOUT THIS

Create a document in Microsoft Paint. Then use 'Save As …' to save it in other file formats such as GIF, JPEG, PNG and so on. Investigate how the quality of the image and the file sizes change for each file format.

DIGITISED SOUND DATA

FILE FORMATS

PCM (Pulse Code Modulation)

This is a technique for capturing sound data by converting the analogue sound data into digital data by encoding the data into a limited number of pulse amplitudes.

RAW

Sound files in PCM format are called RAW because the file has not been compressed or processed further. RAW files can therefore be very large, since there is no compression.

RIFF (Resource Interchange File Format)

This file format is used to store multimedia data (graphics, video and sound) on a computer system.

The RIFF format used to store digital sound data is called WAV (Waveform Audio).

ADPCM (Adaptive Delta Pulse Code Modulation)

RIFF and WAV both use a technique called ADPCM to compress PCM values. ADPCM works by storing the changes in the sample values rather than the sample values themselves. The WAV file format has a compression ratio of 4:1.

MP3

This is a 'lossy' file compression format which is not too harmful in the reduction in quality of the sound. MP3 files have a high compression factor, and this coupled with the little loss of quality has resulted in its widespread commercial use.

The compression works by:

1 removing sounds that are inaudible to the human ear

2 when two similar sounds occur at the same time, the quieter sound is removed.

BIT RATE AND NORMALISATION

Bit rate

Different sound files require a certain number of bits per second to transmit the file. For example, MP3 files have a bit rate of 384 Kbps (kilobits per second).

Normalisation

When sound files are recorded, very often some sounds may be too loud or too quiet. Normalisation is the process of adjusting sound levels so that they are nearer the average volume level of all the sounds.

DON'T FORGET

In general, the size of a sound file can be calculated from the formula:
File size = [Time in seconds] × [Sampling frequency] × [Sampling depth] × [Number of channels].

CALCULATION OF FILE SIZE

The size of a sound file is determined by the following factors:

1 the length of the file in seconds

2 the sampling frequency (how many times per second the sound is sampled)

3 the sample depth (how many bits are used to store each sample)

4 the number of channels (mono is one channel, stereo is two channels).

contd

CALCULATION OF FILE SIZE contd

Example

Calculate the file size of a three-minute audio clip recorded in stereo with a sampling frequency of 44.1 KHz and a sampling depth of 16 bits.

File size
$= 180 \times 44\ 100 \times 16$ bits $\times 2 = 254\ 016\ 000$ bits $= 254\ 016\ 000/8$ bytes $= 31\ 752\ 000$ bytes $= 30.3$ Mb.

CLIPPING, STEREO, SURROUND SOUND AND FADE

Clipping

Sound is recorded up to a certain level of volume. If the sound to be recorded is at too high a volume, then the sound wave will be clipped, which means that the top of the sound wave is cut off. Clipping can result in parts of the sound being unclear or missing.

Stereo

This is sound that has been recorded on two channels by two separate microphones to give a more realistic and wider dimension to the sound.

Surround Sound

This is where several speakers are used to encircle the listener with sound. Surround sound can be used to give the impression that sound is coming from different locations and generally immerse the listener in a more lifelike environment of sound.

Fade

Fading is to gradually reduce the volume of a sound until it dies out. Sound editors have control over the length of the fadeout and how quickly the sound drops in volume.

 Look up specifications of different sound cards on the website www.pcworld.co.uk

SOUND CARDS

A sound card is a circuit board that is used to record and play back sound data on a computer system.

It has a dedicated co-processor and additional RAM to relieve the main processor and memory.

A sound card has the following features:

1 A DSP (Digital Signal Processor) to allow hardware decoding of sound files.

2 Additional RAM to store the sound data.

3 ADC (Analogue-to-Digital Conversion) to convert analogue sound data from a microphone into a form that can be input into a computer.

4 DAC (Digital-to-Analogue Conversion) to convert digital sound data into a form that can be output to speakers.

LET'S THINK ABOUT THIS

There are similarities between graphics cards and sound cards in that they both have a Digital Signal Processor and additional RAM and perform A-to-D and D-to-A conversion.

The calculation of the file size of a sound file is commonly asked for in the exam. Learn this calculation, and there is a good chance that you will pick up some easy marks in the exam.

VECTOR GRAPHICS DATA AND SYNTHESISED SOUND DATA

DON'T FORGET

Vector graphics are also known as object-oriented graphics because the image is stored as a description of a list of layered objects, as opposed to bit-map graphics, which stores an image by colour codes for a two-dimensional array of pixels.

VECTOR GRAPHICS

This topic was covered earlier in the Computer Systems unit in Data Representation 2, but it will now be dealt with in further detail.

In vector graphics, the image is stored as a list of objects and their attributes. Each object is stored independently and can be moved, scaled, brought to the front, edited and so on independently of the other objects in the image.

For example, an image that is made up of a rectangle, circle and line could be stored with the following objects and their attributes:

Rectangle: start x, start y, length, breadth, fill colour, line colour, layer, rotation and so on.
Circle: centre x, centre y, radius, fill colour, line colour, layer, rotation and so on.
Line: start x, start y, end x, end y, line colour, line thickness, layer, rotation and so on.

Layer

Each object has a layer number which specifies how the different objects overlap each other. The vector graphics software will allow objects to be moved to the front and back by changing the layer number. This cannot be done in bit-map graphics, where the image is stored not as individual objects but as an array of pixels.

In the picture below, the layer attributes of the rectangle, circle and line objects have been changed.

Rescaling

The size of vector graphics objects can be enlarged without becoming jagged, since the image is resolution-independent. The attributes are simply changed to reflect the change in size of the object.

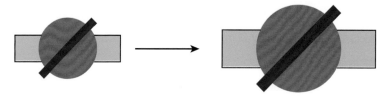

Rotation

The objects in a vector graphics document can be rotated through an angle which is specified by an angle-of-rotation attribute.

File Size

Vector graphics file sizes depend upon the number of objects in the image, unlike bit-map graphics, which must store the colour of each pixel even if large areas are the same colour. Therefore, in general, vector graphics have a very much smaller file size than bit-map graphics, but the file size of vector graphics grows with each object added, whereas the file size of bit-map graphics is set when the document is created.

3D VECTOR GRAPHICS

Vector graphics packages provide three-dimensional objects such as cuboids, spheres and cylinders. These three-dimensional objects have the attributes of shape, position and size but also require attributes additional to those required for two-dimensional objects.

Additional attributes:

1 Surface texture, to give surface definition.
2 Shadow, to simulate the direction of lighting.
3 Z co-ordinate, to specify the third dimension of the object.
4 Angle of rotation, to view the object in different 3D orientations.

FILE FORMATS FOR VECTOR GRAPHICS

Most vector graphics packages have their own way of storing the objects and their attributes, but a few standard file formats exist which are commonly used.

SVG (Scalable Vector Graphics) is a language for describing two-dimensional vector graphics.
VRML (Video Reality Markup/Modelling Language) is used for animations and 3D imaging by describing a scene by attributes.
WRL (World Description Language) is another language used to model 3D scenes.

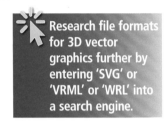

Research file formats for 3D vector graphics further by entering 'SVG' or 'VRML' or 'WRL' into a search engine.

MIDI (MUSICAL INSTRUMENT DIGITAL INTERFACE)

A MIDI interface allows synthesised music that is played on a MIDI instrument to be recorded on a computer system, where it can be edited and played back. The notes that are input into the computer are stored with the following attributes:

Instrument: the MIDI keyboard can make different sounds to represent different instruments. This attribute is used to specify which instrument is to play the note.
Pitch: the frequency of a note (how high or low the note is).
Volume: the amplitude of a note (how loud a note is played).
Duration: the length of time a note lasts.
Tempo: the speed at which the music is played.

ADVANTAGES AND DISADVANTAGES OF MIDI

Advantages

1 MIDI files are smaller than digital sound files.
2 Individual notes can be edited and have effects applied.
3 There is no background noise.

Disadvantages

1 The sound is not as realistic as digital sound files.
2 It cannot deal with vocals.
3 Browsers can't play MIDI files without a plugin.

LET'S THINK ABOUT THIS

Open an application package with drawing tools (vector graphics), create an object and then 'Save' the file. Repeatedly add more objects to the document and use 'Save As …' to save different files for the document as you increase the number of objects. Investigate how the file size changes as the number of objects in the document increases.

The music department in your school will almost certainly have a MIDI instrument. Take an opportunity to get a demonstration of its features.

VIDEO DATA

INTRODUCTION

Video is a sequence of frames displayed in rapid succession to simulate movement.

Frame rate: typically, a frame rate of 25 frames per second is sufficient to create smooth motion.

Bit depth: the number of bits allocated to encode the colour of each pixel.

Resolution: this is measured either in dots per inch (dpi) or by describing the dimension of a frame in pixels, for example 768 × 576.

DON'T FORGET

The bit depth and the resolution of a single video frame is equivalent to the bit depth and resolution of a still bit-map image. Think of video as being a series of bit-map images.

HARDWARE

Video can be captured using an analogue or digital video camera or a web cam.

Digital Video Camera

A digital video camera has a two-dimensional array of charge coupled devices (CCDs) which capture the light and convert it into analogue electrical signals. The analogue signals are then converted to digital data by an analogue-to-digital converter (ADC). A DSP (Digital Signal Processor) adjusts brightness, contrast levels and so on, and compresses the file. The compressed file is then saved onto a backing store device such as a flash card or disc.

Analogue Video Camera

Video can be taken using an analogue video camera, but a video capture card is required to convert the analogue data into a digital form that can be input into a computer system. The card will also have a DSP to perform hardware encoding of data streams into a compressed format such as MPEG (see below).

Web Cam

Video data can be captured with a web cam, which also uses an array of CCDs.

FILE FORMAT

Compressed Techniques

Intraframe compression
This technique compresses each individual frame typically into 'lossy' JPEG format.

Interframe compression
This technique does not store all of the frames. It stores key frames (typically every 10th to 15th frame) and then stores only the changes compared to the key frame in subsequent frames.

AVI (Audio Video Interleave)

This video file format supports a maximum frame rate of 30 frames per second and a resolution of 320 × 240 pixels per frame. AVI files do not have built-in compression.

MPEG (Motion Picture Experts Group)

This format is the standard file format for DVDs, mainly because it has a high compression ratio. This file format stores a few key frames as compressed JPEGs. Subsequent frames after a key frame are compared to the key frame, and only the changes are saved.

Find out more about other video file formats such as MOV and DV (Digital Video) on the internet.

REDUCING FILE SIZE

Video files can be extremely large, so that often it is necessary to reduce size. Apart from compression, the following techniques can be used to reduce video file size.

1 Reduce the frame rate, so that fewer frames are required to be stored.
2 Reduce the bit depth, which results in fewer colours.
3 Reduce the resolution, which reduces the number of pixels in each frame.
4 Crop each frame by trimming the horizontal and vertical edges.

CALCULATION OF FILE SIZE

The size of a video file is determined by the following factors:

1 the length of the file in seconds
2 the frame rate (how many frames are stored per second)
3 the number of pixels in one frame
4 the bit depth.

Example

Calculate the uncompressed file size of an 18-second video clip, captured at 25 frames per second with a resolution of 640 x 480 and 24-bit colour.

File size = 18 × 25 × 640 × 480 × 24 = 3 317 760 000 bits = 414 720 000 bytes = 395.5 Mb.

DON'T FORGET

In general, the size of a video file can be calculated from the formula:
File size = [Time in seconds] × [Frames per second] × [Number of pixels in one frame] × [Bit depth].

VIDEO-EDITING SOFTWARE

Multiple clips can be linked together and edited using video-editing software. Narration can be added, sections can be cropped, audio levels adjusted and so on. Video-editing software has the following features:

Timeline: allows clips to be placed, edited and removed to specify the order and timing in which they are played.

Transition: controls what happens as the video plays from one clip to another.
Examples of transitions are dissolve, fade and page turn.

Sequencing: allows the clips to be moved around on the timeline to change the order in which they are played.

VIDEO CARDS

Video card is another name for a graphics card which manages the display on the screen. The tasks performed by a graphics/video card were previously described in the Bit-mapped Graphics data topic. With respect to video data, a video card has a DSP to allow the hardware decoding of video data streams. For example, the DSP would carry out the decompression of MPEG files.

Bit Rate

The term 'bit rate' is used to describe the amount of video data that can be transmitted by a video card, measured in Mbps (megabits per second) or Kbps (kilobits per second).

LET'S THINK ABOUT THIS

The calculation of file size is similar for graphics, sound and video files. You will almost certainly be asked for at least one of these calculations in the exam. Find out what video-editing software packages are available through computing magazines and the internet, and compare their features.

DEVELOPMENTS IN TECHNOLOGY

CONVERGENT TECHNOLOGY

The term **convergent technology** refers to several multimedia technology functions being provided in a single device. An example of convergent technology is digital TV, which provides the functions of interactive television, internet access, e-mail, game-playing and so on. Other examples are mobile phones, PDAs, games consoles and so on.

COMMUNICATIONS

> **DON'T FORGET**
>
> USB is a 'plug and play' connection, which means that the device is simply connected and used without any configuration or setup requirements.

Clearly, since multimedia files are very large, a high-speed data-transfer rate is required to support multimedia applications. Developments in this area include interfaces with faster and faster transfer rates, and wireless connections.

USB (Universal Serial Bus)

The USB port on a computer can be used to connect scanners, digital cameras and other multimedia peripherals. A USB connection has a maximum transfer rate of 12 megabits per second.

USB2 (Universal Serial Bus 2)

This upgraded version of USB supports a maximum transfer rate of 480 Mbps.

Firewire

This is a high-speed serial bus connection used to connect multimedia devices to a computer system, such as digital camcorder, scanner, audio equipment and so on. Firewire can deliver a bit rate of 800 Mbps.

Wireless Communication

Bluetooth
This wireless connection (radio waves) has a limited transfer range (10 metres) and relatively slow transmission speed but is convenient for transferring data between computers and other devices in a less cluttered environment.

Wi-Fi
This wireless connection has a higher bandwidth and greater range than Bluetooth and has made the internet available in sites such as airports, hotels and coffee shops.

STORAGE TECHNOLOGIES

Decreasing Cost and Size

The cost of storage devices has come down considerably in recent years at the same time as more compact and portable devices have been developed. A typical digital camera at present would have a memory card with a storage capacity that is over 1000 times more than the hard disc of a desktop computer 10 years ago. The trend is set to continue for the cost to keep on going down and for miniaturisation to increase.

Increased Capacity

The capacity of storage devices has increased dramatically over the last decade. The capacity of storage devices is now measured in gigabytes as opposed to megabytes not so long ago.

Optical

DVDs are commonly used to distribute multimedia applications because they are a high-capacity and portable medium.

contd

STORAGE TECHNOLOGIES contd

Magnetic

Floppy discs have virtually disappeared because of their low capacity, and most users prefer to use a memory stick instead. High-capacity hard discs are still the standard for desktop and laptop computers to act as the main backing store.

Holographic

This technology records data in layers right through the full depth of the medium, and not just on the surface as is the case with conventional storage mediums.

The advantages of **holographic storage** are:

1 a very fast access speed, because millions of bits can be written or read in parallel in a single operation

2 a high storage capacity, which makes it suitable to act as a storage device in multimedia applications.

PROCESSOR AND RAM

Faster processor speeds and increased RAM have allowed the development of multimedia applications. Processor clock speeds and RAM capacities of desktop computers have tended to double every year or two.

> Use the internet to research the typical processor clock speeds and RAM capacities of current desktop, laptop and palmtop computers.

DISPLAY TECHNOLOGIES

Flat-panel displays have replaced the bulky cathode-ray tube monitors. The technology to produce 3D displays is advancing to allow objects to be displayed as expected in real life and to be viewed from different angles.

Flat Displays

These exist in the form of TFT (Thin Film Transistor) and LCD (Liquid Crystal Display) displays. TFT screens produce a sharper image than LCD screens.

Virtual 3D Displays

These are 3D displays that are used to produce the 'world' that the user sees in a virtual-reality system. The 3D effect can be created by using two monitors to show a different perspective for each eye in a virtual-reality helmet.

Real 3D Displays

3D displays produce a 3D image without the need for a virtual-reality helmet or special glasses. These displays use some physical mechanism to display points of light within a volume of space. 3D displays include multiplanar displays, which have multiple displays stacked up in planes, and rotating panel displays, where a rotating panel sweeps out a volume.

LET'S THINK ABOUT THIS

The multimedia devices that you have studied in this unit will help you in the Higher coursework task, where in Part 2 you are required to select hardware devices to meet the requirements of a situation and justify your choice. Very often, this task is set in a multimedia scenario such as producing a glossy catalogue.

Conversion programs are available that convert multimedia files from one format into another – for example, WAV sound files into MP3. Look for freeware on the internet that carries out these tasks.

EXAM-STYLE QUESTIONS

DON'T FORGET

These questions are based on the work of the Multimedia Technology unit. Of course, five questions cannot cover the entire syllabus, and you should make good use of past exam papers for your exam preparation.

QUESTION 1

WebsAreUs is a company that produces websites for commercial and educational organisations. New recruits with no experience of web-page creation are trained on a WYSIWYG editor for six months, after which they use a mixture of a text editor and the WYSIWYG editor.

(a) (i) What does WYSIWYG stand for?

(ii) Why is it easier to train the new recruits on a WYSIWYG editor instead of a text editor?

(b) The company also produces multimedia applications using multimedia authoring software. Describe a method that could be used to design the multimedia application.

(c) One of the recruits has created a variety of 20 multimedia files to be used in the multimedia application. Give **two** reasons why a container file would be useful in this situation.

(2, 2, 2)

QUESTION 2

Wendy uses a digital camera to take the picture of a child shown below. The image is then imported into a painting package, where it is saved in 24-bit colour with a resolution of 1200 dpi.

(a) Explain in detail how a digital camera captures graphics data.

(b) The image is compressed before being sent over the internet to friends around the world.
(i) Name a compression method which is suitable for this image.
(ii) Describe how this compression method works.

(3, 3)

QUESTION 3

Winston is interested in birdwatching and has recorded some audio clips of birdsongs. He uses digital sound-editing software to edit the clips, which will be imported into a multimedia presentation package.

(a) One of the audio clips for an osprey lasts for 40 seconds. It is sampled at 24 KHz with a sampling depth of 16 bits in stereo.
Calculate the file size of this audio clip in an appropriate unit.

(b) Winston normalises some of the sound clips.
Why is normalisation of sound files sometimes necessary?

(c) The digital sound-editing software is used to make the audio clips **fade** before they are used in the presentation. Explain the term 'fade'.

(3, 2, 1)

QUESTION 4

Video files can be reduced in size by applying compression techniques. Some file formats for video use 'lossy' compression techniques while others use 'lossless' compression techniques.

(a) **(i)** What is the difference between lossy and lossless compression?

(ii) Describe what is meant by interframe compression.

(b) Give **two** techniques, other than compression, for reducing the size of video files.

(4, 2)

QUESTION 5

Technology developments have contributed to the advancement of multimedia technology. Two key areas of progress are wireless communication and the storage of data.

(a) Two wireless transmission methods are Wi-Fi and Bluetooth.
Give **two** advantages of Wi-Fi over Bluetooth.

(b) A recent development in data storage is holographic storage.
(i) Give a brief description of how data is stored in holographic technology.
(ii) Give **two** advantages of holographic storage.

(c) What is Firewire used for?

(2, 3, 1)

ANSWERS

ANSWER 1

1 mark	**(a) (i)**	What You See Is What You Get.
1 mark	**(ii)**	A WYSIWYG editor allows for simpler entering, formatting and editing of multimedia elements. The elements are dragged and dropped onto the page without the need for detailed knowledge of HTML code that would be required to use a text editor.
1 mark	**(b)**	Storyboarding.
1 mark for description		Storyboarding contains details of the multimedia elements of each screen and their layout, specifies links between screens and so on.
2 × 1 mark for each reason	**(c)**	A container file stores compressed files, which will take up less space. All of the files are stored together in one compressed file, which makes them easy to manage.

ANSWER 2

3 × 1 mark for each point	**(a)**	A rectangular array of CCD sensors captures the image. Each CCD captures the light for a single pixel. An ADC converts the analogue signal to digital.
1 mark	**(b) (i)**	RLE or LZW.
2 marks for good description	**(ii)**	RLE – the colour codes for repeated coloured pixels are stored, as are the number of repeats. **Or** LZW – repeated patterns are given an index, and the index is stored instead of the pattern.

ANSWER 3

3 marks	**(a)**	The storage requirements = 40 × 24 000 × 16 bits × 2 = 30 720 000 bits = 3 840 000 bytes. = 3.7 Mb.
2 marks for good explanation	**(b)**	Some sounds may be too loud or too quiet in a recording, so the range of amplitudes is reduced.
1 mark	**(c)**	Fading is to gradually reduce the volume of a sound until it dies out.

ANSWER 4

(a) (i) Lossy compression is where some of the detail is lost in the compressed file.
Lossless compression is where none of the detail of the original is lost.

2 × 1 mark

(ii) Interframe compression works by storing a few key frames and the changes between the key frames instead of storing all the frames.

2 marks for good description

(b) Reduce the bit depth.
Reduce the frame rate.
Reduce the resolution.
Crop or cut the video.

2 × 1 mark for each technique

ANSWER 5

(a) Wi-Fi has a greater range than Bluetooth.
Wi-Fi has a faster bandwidth.

2 × 1 mark for each advantage

(b) (i) Holographic storage records data through the full depth of the medium instead of only recording on the surface.

1 mark

(ii) Very fast access speed to the data.
Large storage capacity.

2 × 1 mark for each advantage

(c) Firewire is an interface used for connecting multimedia equipment to a computer system.

1 mark

COURSEWORK TASK

OUTLINE AND GUIDANCE

INTRODUCTION

DON'T FORGET

Don't get too worked up about the time allowed for the coursework task. The task is expected to take between 8 and 10 hours, but you will be allowed longer than this if required.

The coursework component for the course consists of a practical task which involves the integration of the practical skills and knowledge developed in the **two compulsory units Computer Systems** and **Software Development**. The optional unit is not assessed in the coursework task.

You will be required to solve a problem in a real-life situation, for which you must produce software and recommend **hardware** devices.

Time Allocation

The task has been designed to be completed by a typical candidate in 8–10 hours. The time allocation is intended to cover the amount of time required to implement and write up your solution. However, there is nothing to stop you researching materials for the task at home.

DON'T FORGET

The coursework task will almost certainly require the use of a function. Remember: a function is a subroutine that returns a single value such as a highest mark or an average. Make sure that you use a function where it is required, or else you will lose marks.

MARKS AND SECTIONS

The coursework task makes up 30 per cent of the overall marks for the course. It is marked out of 60, which is then combined with the exam mark out of 140.

There are **two** sections:

Part 1:   30 marks

This section involves the design, implementation, testing and evaluation of a short but non-trivial program. You will be given the top-level algorithm on which to base the implementation of the program.

The design requires you to use pseudocode to show the detailed logic of the program.

The program requires the use of procedures and functions with parameter passing. Make sure that you can do this in the high-level language that you use.

Part 2:   30 marks

This section involves the selection of actual hardware devices to meet the requirements of a typical task with a budget of a few thousand pounds. Typically, you will have to consider four devices.

For each device, you have to identify two actual devices and compare them in terms of characteristics such as speed, accuracy, capacity and cost. Then you must choose which of the two devices better meets the requirements of the task, and justify your choice.

The hardware devices for the coursework task will change from year to year, but it is worth noting that devices such as printers, scanners, digital cameras, screen displays and digital camcorders are commonly asked for.

Also, the specification and cost of desktop and laptop computers is often a requirement of the hardware section.

PREPARATION

The coursework task changes each session, but there is a lot of similarity each year in the requirements. The tasks for previous years are readily available from the SQA website, or your teacher should be able to give you copies. Study these tasks to get a feel for what is being expected of you and recognise patterns from year to year.

 Look up information on the coursework task on the SQA website www.sqa.org.uk

MARKING SCHEME

Your teacher will give you a copy of the coursework marking scheme. It is this document that the teacher strictly follows when marking your work – so, make sure that you meet all the requirements that are detailed in this document.

The marking scheme takes into account any assistance given to the student to complete the task, and marks will be deducted if you are given too much help. So, do not seek help at the first sign of difficulty but be prepared to persevere with a problem.

Of course, if you are completely stuck, do seek help, since the completion of later tasks can be based upon earlier tasks. For example, you cannot gain the marks for testing your software until you have a completed and working program.

The guidelines shown below are used by your teacher to mark your work.
Full marks are awarded if a task is completed successfully without assistance.
1 mark is subtracted if the task is completed with some assistance or hints.
0 marks are awarded if the task is not achieved or if significant assistance is given.

DON'T FORGET

Two marks are given for the 'completeness and clarity of the report'. These are easy marks to pick up; but make sure that your write-up is well presented with a title page, index, page numbers, good layout of text and graphics and so on.

LET'S THINK ABOUT THIS

The coursework task is an assessment of your practical knowledge and skills, but remember that it is the write-up where marks are gained and lost. Think about the layout and the presentation of your write-up.

Study the marking scheme and make sure that you have met all the requirements before you hand in your documentation.

Last thoughts.
Talk to sixth-formers in your school who did Higher Computing last year. Ask them for advice about tackling the exam and the coursework task and any difficulties to expect.

INDEX

Accumulator (A) data register 12
actual program parameters 57
adaptive maintenance 48
ADC (Analogue-to-Digital Conversion) 106
address bus 12, 14
ADPCM (Adaptive Delta Pulse Code Modulation) technique 108
adressability 13
ADSL (Asymmetric Digital Subscriber Line) 99
algorithms, standard 58
ALU (Arithmetic and Logic Unit) 12
analysis, system 38–9
ANS (Artificial Neural Systems) 68
anti-aliasing graphics 107
anti-virus software 90–1
anti-virus utilities 21, 23
application-based performance testing 14
array data structure 54, 57
Artificial Intelligence 64
ASCII system 8
asynchronous data transmission 92–3
AVI (Audio Video Interleave) file format 112

backing store devices 11
backtracking 75
backup server 91
backup strategies 91
bandwidth 19, 98
benchmark programs 14
binary number system 6, 10
BIOS (Basic Input/Output System) 11
bit depth 8, 24, 107, 112
bit rate 108, 113
bit-mapped graphics 8–9, 106
bluetooth connection 114
boolean data type 54
boot-sector virus 23
bootstrap loader 20
breadth first searching 72-3
broadband internet connection 99
browser programs 84
buffering 15
bus topology 18

cache memory 15
CCD (Charged Coupled Device) 106
CD-ROM (Compact Disc Read-Only Memory) storage device 29

censorship 87
character data type 54
Chatterbots program 67
checksum 23, 93
circuit switching 95
client/server network 16
clipping of sound waves 109
clock speed of processors 14
codec files 105
combinatorial explosion 73
command-language interpreter 20
compilers 53
compression techniques 9, 21, 106–7
Computer Misuse Act 19, 87
container files 105
control bus 12–13
control constructs 50
control unit 12
Copyright and Patents Act 19, 87
corrective maintenance 48
counting occurrences algorithm 58
CPU (Central Processing Unit) 10, 12
CRC (Cyclic Redundancy Check) 93
CSMA/CD (Carrier Sense Multiple Access Collision Detection) 94

data bus 12, 14
data format conversion 15
Data Protection Act 19, 87
data transmission 92–5
data types 54
declarative languages 51, 66, 74
defragmenter 21
denial-of-service attack 88–9
depth first searching 72–3
design, system 40
dialup internet connection 98
digital camera input device 23–4, 106, 112
direct access 28
disc repair 21
display technologies 115
dithering graphics technique 107
DNS (Domain Name Service) 83
documentation of software system 47
domain name 83
DVD (Digital Versatile Disc) storage device 29
dynamic RAM 11

e-commerce 86–7
Eliza program 66–7
embedded files 105
EPROM (Erasable Programmable Read-Only Memory) 11
error-checking during data transmission 93
ethernet 94
evaluation of software 47
event-driven languages 52
expert systems 70–1

fault-tolerance components 91
fetch-execute cycle 13
file compression 9, 21, 106–7, 112, 113
file formats 106–7, 108–9, 110–11, 112
file management 20
file virus 22
firewalls 90
firewire bus connection 114
flat screen output device 27
floating-point numbers 7
floppy disc drive storage device 28
FLOPS (Floating-Point Operations Per Second) 14
formal program parameters 57
FTP (File Transfer Protocol) 80
function, program 56

game-playing programs 66
GIF (Graphics Interchange Format) file format 21, 106–7
gigabyte (Gb) 6
global variables 56
GPU (Graphics Processing Unit) 107
graphic representation 8–9
graphic resolution 8, 107, 112
graphics card 107

hard disc drive storage device 28
heuristics 73
high-level programming languages 50
HTML (Hypertext Markup Language) 84, 105
HTTP (Hypertext Transfer Protocol) 80, 85
HTTPS (HTTP over Secure socket layer) 86
hub, network 17
hyperlink 84

implementation, system 42
inheritance 74

inkjet printer output device 26
input devices 24–5
instantiation 75
Instruction Register (IR) 12
integer data type 54
integers 6–7
intelligent robots 70
interface 15
internal program comments 42
internet 16
internet filtering software 90
interpreters 53
intranet 16
IP addresses 82
IP (Internet Protocol) 17, 81, 83
ISDN (Integrated Service Digital Network) 98
ISP (Internet Service Provider) 82
iteration 37

JPEG (Joint Photographic Expert Group) file format 21, 107

keyboard input device 24
kilobyte (Kb) 6
knowledge base 51, 74
knowledge representation 65

LAN (Local-Area Network) 16
language processing 66–7
laser printer output device 26
leased line internet connection 99
legal acts 19, 87
linear search algorithm 58
LISP programming language 66
local variables 56
logic programming 66
logical error 44

macro virus 22
macros 52
magnetic tape storage device 28–9
mainframe computers 16
maintenance of software 48–9
manual trace 74–5
megabyte (Mb) 6
memory capacity 13
memory management 20
memory read and write operations 13

mesh topology 18
microbrowser programs 84
MIDI (Musical Instrument Digital Interface) 111
minimum/maximum algorithm 59
MIPS (Millions of Instructions Per Second) 14
mirror discs 91
module independence 49
module library 53
MPEG (Motion Picture Experts Group) file format 112
multimedia application development 104–5
multiscan monitor output device 27

natural language processing 66–7
negation 74
network protocols 80–1
network security 88–9
network switching 95
networks 16–17
NIC (Network Interface Card) 17
NLP (Natural Language Processing) 69
normalisation of sound levels 108

operating system 20–1, 22
OSI (Open Systems Interconnection) model 80–1
output devices 26–7

packet switching 95
packets, network 17
parallel interface 15
parallel processing 67, 73
parameters, program 57
parity check 8, 93
passing parameters 57
PCM (Pulse Code Modulation) file format 108
peer-to-peer network 16–17
perfective maintenance 48
performance measures
    14–15
peripheral devices 11, 24
personal privacy 87
personnel, software 37
pinging 89
PNG (Portable Network Graphics) file format 107
procedural languages 50–1, 66
procedure, program 56
process management (kernel) 21
processor buses 12–13
processor registers 12

Program Counter (PC) register 12
programming language 44
Prolog programming language 66, 74
PROM (Programmable Read-Only Memory) 11
protocols, network 80
proxy server 90
pseudocode 41, 47

RAID (Random Array of Inexpensive Discs) 91
RAM (Random Access Memory) 10, 22, 115
RAW sound files 108
real data type 54
real numbers 7
recursion 51, 74
registers 12
Regulation of Investigatory Powers Act (2000) 87
repeater, network 17
repetition (iteration) control construct 50
resolution, graphics 8, 107, 112
restricted domain 65
RGB colour codes 107
RIFF (Resource Interchange File Format) 108
ring topology 18
robots, intelligent 70
ROM (Read-Only Memory) 10–11, 20
router, network 17
run-time error 44

scanner input device 24, 106
scripting languages 52
search engines 85
search techniques 72–3
security measures on internet 86
security measures on networks 88–9
Select Case statement 55
selection (branching) control construct 50
semantic nets 65
sequencing control construct 50
sequential access 28
serial interface 15
SHRDLU program 67
smart/embedded technology 70
SMTP (Simple Mail Transfer Protocol) 80
software compatibility 22
software development process 36
software specification 39
sound cards 25, 109
sound data files 108–9

spooling 15
SSSD (Solid-State Storage Devices) 29
star topology 18
static RAM 11
stereo sound 109
storage devices 28–9, 114–15
Stored Program Concept 10
streaming data 105
string data type 54
string operations 54–5
structure diagram 40–1, 47
structured walkthrough 44
subgoal 74, 75
surround sound 109
SVG (Scalable Vector Graphics) file format 111
switch, network 17
synchronous data transmission 92–3
syntax error 44
system performance 14

tape backups 91
TCP (Transmission Control Protocol) 81, 83
TCP/IP protocol 82–3
technical guidess, writing 46
teleworking 86–7
telnet protocol 80
testing, systematic 44–5
text representation 8
top-down software design 40
topology, network 18
transmission media 19
Trojan horse 22
Turing test 64–5
two-state devices 10
two's complement number system 6–7

Unicode system 8
UPS (Uninterrupted Power Supply) 91
URL (Universal Resource Locator) 80
USB (Universal Serial Bus) 114
user guides, writing 46
user interface design 40
utility programs 21

variables, program 54, 56
vector graphics 9, 110–11
video cards 25, 113
video data 112–13
video-editing software 113
virus, computer 22–3
virus signature 23
vision systems 68–9
VRML (Video Reality Markup/Modelling Language)
    file format 111

walled garden 90
WAN (Wide-Area Network) 16
WAP (Wireless Application Protocol) 84–5
web cam 112
web pages development 105
wi-fi connection 114
wireless networks 96–7
WLAN (Wireless Local Area Network) 97
WML (Wireless Markup Language) 84–5
wordsize 12
worm 22
WPAN (Wireless Personal Area Network) 96
WRL (World Description Language) file format 111
WWAN (Wireless Wide Area Network) 97
WYSIWYG editors 105